RICHARD MAURICE BUCKE, medical mystic

Richard Maurice Bucke

Walt Whitman

—When one is ill, doctors are most depressing.

—Bucke's
not that breed: he tends the mad, in Canada—
a kind of medical mystic
he lets me call him

Richard Howard
Wildflowers

RICHARD MAURICE BUCKE, medical mystic

Letters of Dr. Bucke to Walt Whitman and His Friends

selected and edited by
ARTEM LOZYNSKY
Temple University

with a Foreword by Gay Wilson Allen

Wayne State University Press   Detroit   1977

Library of Congress Cataloging in Publication Data

Bucke, Richard Maurice, 1837–1902.
  Richard Maurice Bucke, medical mystic.

  Includes index.
  1. Whitman, Walt, 1819–1892—Correspondence.
2. Bucke, Richard Maurice, 1837–1902. 3. Poets,
American—19th century—Correspondence. 4. Physicians—
Canada—Correspondence. I. Whitman, Walt, 1819–1892.
II. Lozynsky, Artem, 1941–   III. Title.
PS3231.A34   1977b   811'.3   77-6818
ISBN 0-8143-1576-3

to my parents

contents

foreword

Gay Wilson Allen

The first biography of Walt Whitman, published in 1883 by the Canadian psychiatrist (then called "alienist") Dr. Richard Maurice Bucke, has caused great controversy. The poet admitted that he wrote part of it, an admission which the holograph manuscripts confirm, and most recent critics have assumed that Whitman's main concern in the collaboration was to influence posterity to accept his exalted evaluation of himself. However, in studying the correspondence of Whitman and Bucke, Artem Lozynsky finds that the poet actually tried to curb his friend's fanaticism. He loved praise (what poet does not?), but he objected to being regarded as a "god."

If Lozynsky had done no more than show us that Whitman tried to restrain Dr. Bucke's ardor, his work would be justified. But he has done a great deal more. Perhaps most important, he reveals Bucke's interpretation of Whitman as religious, not literary. Readers might have guessed this from Bucke's biography of Whitman and from his *Cosmic Consciousness*, in which he cites the author of *Leaves of Grass* as representative of a new type of humanity with a "cosmic" mind. *Cosmic Consciousness* has been reprinted scores of times, and it still sells. Today Whitman's literary reputation is secure, but he also has a strong subterranean cultist appeal in various parts of the world which *Cosmic Consciousness* continues to satisfy.

Bucke's significance to Whitman scholars, however, does not rest entirely on his having been the first of Whitman's biographers to offer a "mystical" interpretation of the poet. He was also one of Whitman's three literary executors, who edited the so-called *Complete Writings* (though actually far from complete) published in 1902 in ten volumes. Bucke himself also edited *Calamus* (Whitman's letters to Peter Doyle), the *Wound-Dresser* (Civil War letters), and *Notes and Fragments* (a collection drawn from unpublished manuscripts).

Lozynsky's original intention was to put together a complete, thoroughly annotated edition of Bucke's letters to Whitman and to some of the poet's friends. However, to publish these many and sometimes mundane letters in one volume seemed impractical, and there was the danger, as well, that in such an edition the more important, interesting, and readable ones might get lost in the mass. He therefore decided to expand his critical and biographical remarks and to use them to introduce the generous samples of the letters which we have here in *Richard Maurice Bucke, Medical Mystic*. At the same time Lozynsky has made the complete correspondence available to scholars in *The Let-*

ters of Dr. Richard Maurice Bucke to Walt Whitman, presently on microfilm and published on demand. I think that this plan was a wise one on the part of author and publisher—perfect, in fact—and highly recommend both collections.

Medical Mystic will, of course, receive more critical attention and will be more widely used than the volume containing the complete collection. Knowing Whitman was the great experience of Bucke's life, and we see here how he repaid his debt by helping to make the old man's last years of life more comfortable and by the most devout effort, after his death, to erect literary monuments to his memory. Lozynsky shows Bucke in all his quirky, humane, sympathetic reality. I feel that Dr. Richard Maurice Bucke has indeed been lucky to find so competent a biographer, critic, and editor.

preface

Because the published writings of Dr. Richard Maurice Bucke have been neglected and most of his letters remain unpublished, his career as Walt Whitman's most ardent disciple has been misunderstood. He has been regarded as merely the 'hottest' of what Bliss Perry has called Whitman's 'hot little prophets'. The systematic examination of his books and letters to Whitman and Whitman's disciples presented here, however, reveals that Bucke's devotion was sparked and sustained by 'cosmic consciousness'—his term for a mystical comprehension of the universe.

This study offers critical readings of Bucke's books and provides texts of letters pertinent to them, as well as a chapter of letters documenting his daily activities as physician, literary executor, and disciple. For those who wish to trace Bucke's career as Whitman's disciple in more detail, an annotated edition of his collected letters to Whitman, which also contains a selected bibliography of Bucke's writings, is being published simultaneously with the present volume and is available through the Xerox University Microfilms publishing *On Demand* program.

Arnold L. Goldsmith read the manuscript at an earlier stage and helped to give the study balance. William White allowed me to draw freely on his vast knowledge of Whitman biography and bibliography and made available to me the galleys of his edition of Whitman's 'Commonplace-Book'. Herbert M. Schueller's edition of the letters of John Addington Symonds has provided a model. Without Charles E. Feinberg this study would not have been possible. He has assembled the most significant Whitman collection of this century and has made it freely available to generations of scholars. In the course of my frequent visits to his home I came to regard him not only as Whitman's most dedicated collector but also as one of his disciples.

I am grateful to the following institutions for supplying me with copies of Bucke letters and related materials in their collections: County Borough of Bolton (England) Public Libraries; the Library of Congress, Washington, D.C.; The John Rylands Library, Manchester, England; Syracuse University; and the University of Western Ontario, London, Ontario. I wish to thank, in particular, Gloria A. Francis of the Detroit Public Library and Edward Phelps of the D. B. Weldon Library of the University of Western Ontario. Jean Owen, my editor, has been my 'terrible surgeon'.

Letter 12 first appeared in *Notes and Queries*, 220 (1975), 120–21; letter 37 in *Papers of the Bibliographical Society of America*, 68 (1974), 442–44; letter 47 in the *Walt Whitman Review*, 19 (1973), 28–30, 34; and letter 106 in *American Literature*, 47 (1975), 270–73. I am grateful to the editors of these journals for allowing me to reprint them.

Note on the Texts

Bucke's often eccentric spellings and punctuation have been retained. I have transcribed Bucke's manuscripts letter for letter, employing the following symbols:

editor's insertions are enclosed within brackets

only one Jew [Paul]

Bucke's insertions or additions to the manuscript are enclosed within slashes

photo-intaglio will face /title/ page

a slash in brackets indicates that at this point Bucke used the right-hand margin as an all-purpose punctuation mark

together[/] I then

a dash in brackets indicates that at this point Bucke left extra space within a line to indicate a new paragraph

[—]

single quotation marks are used throughout text, letters, and annotations; all punctuation within these marks is the author's

the text is marked 'copy proof'

double quotation marks appear only where Bucke himself used them in his manuscript

my remarks on "children of Adam"

RICHARD MAURICE BUCKE,

medical mystic

1

Introduction

Real appreciation of Richard Maurice Bucke's letters to Walt Whitman requires some understanding of the circumstances under which they were written. After Whitman's series of strokes in June of 1888, he and Bucke both knew that he was dying—indeed, every few months Bucke would prepare to depart for Camden, positive that Whitman's death was at hand. The illness, however, was lingering and protracted, and, as much as anything, Bucke's motive in writing was simply to stay in touch. His letters to Whitman frequently contain nothing more than trivia, but at times their blandness is deceptive.

Bucke would often write an urgent and anxious letter to Horace Traubel and a leisurely and chatty one to Whitman on the same day. Some of his letters to Traubel indicate that all was not going smoothly within the group of Whitman disciples, but Bucke either avoided discussing these problems in his letters to Whitman or alluded to them only in passing, displaying the smooth bedside manner of the physician.

There is also another and more subtle reason for the general tone and content of the letters of Bucke to Whitman. Whitman did not enjoy writing or receiving 'literary' letters. What he liked were glimpses of commonplace, ordinary life. A comparison of Bucke's letters to his friend Harry Buxton Forman—full of literary and philosophic speculations—with those he wrote to Whitman shows that Bucke suited his style to Whitman's taste.

Bucke's most immediate service to Whitman, however, was that of a physician. He told him that he needed a full-time male nurse, helped Traubel start a fund to pay for one, and even sent Edward Wilkins from London, Ontario, to Camden to serve in that capacity. He arranged for Sir William Osler to examine Whitman and to recommend physicians for him in the Camden-Philadelphia area. From time to time, Bucke would send Whitman a prescription, usually a digestive aid, but what was perhaps most important was that he turned a sympathetic, yet professional, ear to the poet's minute and sustained descriptions of his physical ailments.

Bucke, a book collector, was intensely interested in every aspect of Whitman bibliography, and many letters to Whitman discuss various items which he wished for his collection. Although Whitman was no bibliophile, he gladly supplied Bucke with manuscripts and printed materials, realizing that a comprehensive collection of his work was taking shape.

The greatest value of these letters, however, lies in the indirect narrative they provide of Bucke's attempt to lay the foundations for a new religion. For Bucke, Whitman was far more than a great poet—he was the founder of a new and superior religion. Bucke felt that he was one of the few who appreciated this astounding fact and was concerned with the orderly transfer of authority and doctrine from dying master to living disciples. It was necessary to establish the identity of the true band of believers and to determine the structure of power within that group, and it is especially interesting to note how, in the process of Bucke's efforts, some of Whitman's older disciples, like John Burroughs, were gradually eased out of places of importance in the poet's inner circle. It was also necessary for Bucke to convert the unbelieving, and in some respects his trip to England the year before Whitman died could be called an apostolic journey. However, without some understanding of Bucke's childhood experiences or of the peculiar philosophic system he attempted to work out, much of this devotion to Whitman may appear to be no more than unbridled and flamboyant enthusiasm.

Richard Maurice Bucke was born on 18 March 1837 at Methwold, County of Norfolk, England.[1] His father, the Reverend Horatio Walpole Bucke, was a great-grandson of Sir Robert Walpole and a grand-nephew of Horace Walpole. When Bucke was a year old, the family emigrated to Upper Canada and settled on a farm near London, Ontario. The Reverend Mr. Bucke, who had a reading knowledge of seven languages, brought his library of several thousand volumes to Canada, and it was among these books that the Bucke children educated themselves. Even as a child Bucke was curious about the after-life and other spiritual matters. He later recalled that 'on one occasion when about ten years old he earnestly longed to die that the secrets of the beyond, if there were any beyond, might be revealed to him'.[2] His religious beliefs were always unorthodox. He claimed that 'He never, even as a child, accepted the doctrines of the Christian church; but, as soon as old enough to dwell at all on such themes, conceived that Jesus was a

21

man—great and good no doubt, but a man. That no one would ever be condemned to everlasting pain. That if a conscious God existed he was the supreme master and meant well in the end to all; but that, this visible life here being ended, it was doubtful, or more than doubtful, whether conscious identity would be preserved.'[3]

At the age of sixteen, Bucke left Ontario and headed for the West, eventually reaching California. In the next five years his adventures included fighting off, with a few companions, a band of Shoshone Indians, marching for 150 miles with only a little flour mixed with water to eat, freezing one foot so badly that he had to have it amputated, and coming close to discovering the fabulous Comstock lode.[4] At age twenty-one, in 1858, he returned to Canada and McGill University. He was graduated as a doctor of medicine in 1862. His thesis, 'The Correlation of the Vital and Physical Forces', showing his early interest in the relationship of the spiritual and the physical, won the Governor's Prize and was published.[5] He also won the Professor's Prize in Clinical Medicine for his case reporting.

Bucke then left Canada for two years of study in England and France. A portion of his diary, for the years 1862 to 1866, has survived[6] and provides a record of his day-to-day reading, which was both systematic and extensive. Along with medical books he read philosophy and literature. He read Auguste Comte almost daily, but his most detailed diary notations concern fiction and poetry. Although he read the classics systematically, he reserved his commentaries for contemporary literature. One of his favorite novels was Charles Kingsley's highly romantic *Westward, Ho!*. His entry for 5 May 1863 reads:

> having been itching to get at it all the morning, went into "Amyas Leigh" [the hero of *Westward, Ho!*] along with my lunch & smoke, intending like an honest student to give him up as soon as I had done them [some errands]—but this I found impossible and I stuck to him facinated hour after hour till dinner time, and then again till I finished him about 8 or a little after; it is the very God of

novels, I was wholey carried away by it, far from the dim east and
north once more westward to the most divine land of America,
fairly wallowing in the glorious sunshine & rich vegetation of the
south and west, the wild grandeur of the western wilderness that I
know so well! but must never, never more see except in such
visions—Ye mighty scenes of mountains, river, forest, and lovely
valley how ye passed before me, almost turning my brain with
indescrible feelings of longings, regret, exultation & despair,—to
think to have seen such & never more to see, a cripple, a wreck—

Quite regularly Bucke and his English friends Harry Buxton Forman and Alfred Forman met to read aloud Romantic
and contemporary Victorian verse—chiefly the works of
Shelley and Byron, Tennyson and the Brownings.

When Bucke left England the Forman brothers continued
to keep him up to date on the literary news.[7] Their correspondence continued until Alfred Forman's death and indicates the scope of Bucke's literary interests.

Bucke set up medical practice in Sarnia, Ontario, in
January 1864, and matters seemed to be going well at first.
Early in March, however, he suddenly received two letters
and a telegram from California friends urging him to return
because a lawsuit was being brought against a mining
company there and he was needed as a witness at the trial.
For various reasons the trial was delayed for eight months,
and because of this and other complications Bucke remained in California for fourteen months, supported by a
stipend of $250 a month, plus a lump sum of $2,500, given
him for his contribution to the trial. He practiced a little
medicine but, with this income to support him, devoted
most of his time to reading and to learning German. From
time to time he mused about becoming a writer (he had
written some verse as a student) but came to realize that
his role was to appreciate rather than to create. On 1 July
1864, he made the following entry:

Music and singing in the parlor in the evening—Someone sang an
old song that Fanny P. used to sing when I was in love with her—I
was in my room and leaned out of the window to hear it—in the

mean time looking over the lake—the blending of emotions of the three periods (when I was in California before & saw this lake— when I heard Fanny sing this song, and now) produced a most peculiar state of mind—which could it be well expressed in verse would make a beautifull poem quite in Shelleys style but I am no Shelley and don't think of attempting it—I am feeling myself more & more constrained to give up the notion that there may be possibly some capabilities in me above a fair average of half educated men—the sooner I get entirely rid of such notions, probably the better it will be for me.

Bucke's most notable accomplishment in California was learning to read and to speak German. He hired a German tutor and took a room in the home of a German family to practice the language. In later years, Bucke put his mastery of German in the service of Whitman.

After returning to Sarnia, Bucke revived his medical practice and, in 1865, married. He settled into the routine of the small-town doctor, and the only point of interest in his diary entries in this period is his casual attitude toward Christianity. The following is his entry for Christmas Day of 1865: '—up late—loafed about—George [unidentified] got down between 11 & 12 [/] he and I played poker most of [?] day and evening—greatly as I found to Jessie's disjust and I cannot say I felt proud of my self about it afterwards—I lost a dollar & a half but that is no consequence'. When Bucke attended church, he attended grudgingly. On 15 February 1866, he noted: 'Sunday. To church in morning for first time in four or five weeks and was disjusted at myself for going today but one must give in a little on such points—'.

Bucke stopped making regular diary entries on 4 March 1866: 'it was getting too mechanical. . . . My life also now that I am fairly married and settled down to work is so monotonous that what I said of it one day answers for every other day—and there is therefor [sic] no object in keeping a daily record of my doings,—'. There are only two more entries in the diary, one on 6 March 1866 and the other on 19 October 1868.

It was during this period of his life that Bucke first heard of Walt Whitman. In 'Memories of Walt Whitman' he recalls this incident and the profound effect it had on him:

> I recall as if it were yesterday the first time I ever heard pronounced the name of the author of 'Leaves of Grass.' It was in mid-winter, 1867–8. A friend of mine, who then lived in Montreal, the Mineralogist to the Geological Survey of Canada, a first-class chemist, geologist and scientist generally, T. Sterry Hunt, was visiting me in Sarnia, where I then lived and practiced. One evening . . . Dr. Hunt . . . asked: 'Did you ever hear of a man named Walt Whitman?' I replied: 'No: who is he?' Dr. Hunt answered: 'He is an American poet who writes in a very peculiar style—something between prose and verse.' And he went on to quote all he could recollect—only a line or two—from the 'Leaves.' But there came to me at that moment, upon that mere mention of the poet's name, how conveyed or whence I have not the least notion, a conviction, which never afterwards left me, that the man so named was a quite exceptional person, and that a knowledge of him and of his writings was of peculiar importance to me.[8]

In documenting the early stages of Bucke's discipleship, the letters between him and the Forman brothers are extremely useful. The first letter in which he mentions Whitman is written on 19 February 1869 to Harry Buxton Forman:

> You will have seen the collection of Walt Whitman's Poems that have been edited by Rossetti & published by John Camden Hotten Son, 1868. You will probably have got a copy and taken it home and looked into it, but have you *soaked* through the crust into the heart of it? Have you seen that here is the modern poet? Especially the American poet, and the only one so far, the founder of American literature as Goethe was of German literature? that here at last in the doings of man is something 'consummate with the broadcast doing of day and night'? that here in fact is a master mind in literature—A mind too great to be confined in poems & usages—that makes as it goes ways & forms & usages for generations to come. A mind & heart on a large scale in which there is no littleness, no humbug, no pretense, no make believe[,] which receive with themselves the outside world as it is without warp or refraction and which render it back again without warp or refraction. In fact if I am not mistaken we have here correct revelation—For this is A *man* as he reveals *himself*—.[9]

In his reply, Harry Buxton Forman compares Whitman with Swinburne:

> Your mention of Walt Whitman opens up a subject of steadily growing enthusiasm with me. I have read him a little from a friend's copy, and a good deal from my own copy of Rossetti's edition. Almost all you say I seem to agree with. The "crust" does not repel me though it does not attract like the crust of Swinburne's work; but the *Man* is obviously as noble as the other is ignoble, if we are to judge simply on the heart of each. I think Swinburne has no heart; but is a marvelous agglomeration of sensual and intellectual qualities—a cross between the lesser ape and the greater man with none of the woman element in him which goes to make perfect the tale of every man's endowments; another element which Whitman has largely. He has come upon me with such a sense of greatness that I have not trusted myself to print a word on him, for want of the time to read, mark, learn, and inwardly digest as I feel I must do before delivering an opinion on him. Write me some more about him; what you have written touched me the more that it expresses nobly what I have felt without formulation.[10]

By April Bucke felt that he had arrived at what he believed to be the essence of Whitman and wrote to Harry Buxton Forman:

> The secret of the man is the secret of success in all things—literature and everything else—Truth—*Sincerity*. . . . here is a man who receives images of spiritual and material things from without and transmits them again without the least thought of what will the world say of this idea and how will the world like this form of expression, or into what form did such a great poet cast his thought. He speaks from his own soul with the most perfect candor, sincerity and truth. There is nothing in modern literature like it. This, according to me, is his claim to praise, a claim that must not be distorted. Praise that will live while the English language is read.[11]

Forman was willing to accept Bucke's claim for Whitman's sincerity but raised the common criticism of his propriety. On 14 July 1869, he wrote Bucke: 'Sincerity is stamped on every page—doubtless, but bad-taste according to our notions is stamped on the surface of many pages, and paradox seems to abound'.[12]

In the winter of 1869 Bucke was attempting to encourage Harry Buxton Forman to bring out a complete edition of Whitman in England, and began to collect Whitman's work and to collate the various editions of *Leaves of Grass*. On 12 June 1870, he wrote to Forman: 'I *must* have *all* Walt's writings if I can get them.'[13] In a letter to Forman in April he noted that one of his brothers was helping him with the task of collation: 'Julius helps me emending [i.e., collating] "Walt Whitman" and we have already spent several evenings at it and are not yet half through the poem. The alterations in the 1868 [1867] edition are more numerous and greater than I expected to find them. They are very interesting and often throw light upon the thought.'[14]

In the early 1870s Bucke became ill. It is difficult to determine the nature of his illness, but from his letters to the Forman brothers it appears to have been the result of the effects of the harsh climate of Ontario and overwork. He visited England for a short time in the winter of 1871, that summer, and again in the spring of 1872. Shortly before leaving for England on his third visit, Bucke wrote to Harry Buxton Forman: 'My health has completely broken down again and as I am now satisfied that this is due to the climate here, or rather to the malaria[,] I have decided to pull stakes and leave Sarnia for good.'[15] Although Bucke seemed to hold the climate responsible for his illness, when he returned from his trip he abandoned the practice of medicine for two years to devote himself to land speculation, and in March, after this change of occupation, he was able to write to Forman from Sarnia that his health was 'first-rate'.[16]

During this last visit to England Bucke experienced the illumination which was central to his life. It seems to have occurred in late March or early April. A full account of it, is found in *Cosmic Consciousness*, which he published 29 years later:

It was in the early spring, at the beginning of his thirty-sixth year. He and two friends had spent the evening reading Wordsworth, Shelley, Keats, Browning, and especially Whitman. They parted at midnight, and he had a long drive in a hansom (it was in an English city [London]). His mind, deeply under the influence of the ideas, images and emotions called up by the reading and talk of the evening, was calm and peaceful. He was in a state of quiet, almost passive enjoyment. All at once, without warning of any kind, he found himself wrapped around as it were by a flame-colored cloud. For an instant he thought of fire, some sudden conflagration in the great city; the next, he knew that the light was within himself. Directly afterwards came upon him a sense of exultation, of immense joyousness accompanied or immediately followed by an intellectual illumination quite impossible to describe. Into his brain streamed one momentary lightning-flash of the same Brahmic Splendor which has ever since lighted his life; upon his heart fell one drop of Brahmic Bliss, leaving thence forward for always an aftertaste of heaven. Among other things he did not come to believe, he saw and knew that the Cosmos is not dead matter but a living Presence, that the soul is immortal, that the universe is so built and ordered that without any peradventure all things work together for the good of each and all, that the foundation principle of the world is what we call love and that the happiness of every one is in the long run absolutely certain. He claims that he learned more within the few seconds during which the illumination lasted than in previous months or even years of study, and that he learned much that no study could ever have taught.

The illumination itself continued not more than a few moments, but its effect proved ineffaceable; it was impossible for him ever to forget what he at that time saw and knew; neither did he, or could he, every doubt the truth of what was then presented to his mind. There was no return, that night or at any time, of the experience. He subsequently wrote a book [*Man's Moral Nature*] in which he sought to embody the teaching of the illumination.[17]

Bucke later claimed that the thesis of *Man's Moral Nature* (1879) first came to him in this moment of illumination. From his letters to the Forman brothers, however, it is clear that he had been mulling over moral philosophy as early as the fall of 1871, for in early September of that year he wrote to Harry Buxton Forman: 'I have made a lot of notes on my speculations in moral philosophy or whatever you like to call it, but I shall not be able to do much at it for awhile yet as I have so much else to attend to.'[18] By December Bucke had begun to realize the vast implications of his theory. As he wrote to Forman:

> I am pretty busy with practice and one thing or another and do not get on at all with the development of my philosophical ideas except that some slight mental elaboration is going on pretty much all the time. The thing has occupied my mind a great deal since I saw you and I am more and more impressed with the importance of it, but I almost despair of ever being able to put it into such shape as to make it assimilable for other minds. It is such a confounded big affair I don't feel as if I could handle it. It will be nothing less than a new theory of all art and religion and I am sure a *true* one. It will furnish a sound basis for poetical and other art criticism, not but that taste and ability will be needed to work on this basis. It will supply a new theory of the universe and of men's relations to the external universe and which being as a religion as positive as positivism and will supply more hope for mankind and will not shut up men's faculties in the known and present in the same way that positivism does.[19]

Bucke's moment of illumination may have served more to confirm than to reveal to him man's moral nature.

Upon his return to Sarnia Bucke was certain that he had original ideas about the moral nature, but was unable to formulate them: 'I find it very difficult to put my ideas into an intelligible shape', he wrote to Harry Buxton Forman. 'The ideas themselves are all on hand and have been for several months. I carry them still entirely in my head because I cannot get them out of it unto paper. I have turned and twisted them into all sorts of lights, and I am as much convinced as ever that they are both original and valuable. But whether I shall ever succeed in getting them in such a shape so as to judge them, I do not know.'[20] The next June he wrote to Forman: 'I think I see a truer and deeper explanation of the function of the arts than any that has been propounded yet.'[21] But nearly two years later, he had done little to develop his thesis. On 17 February 1875, he wrote to Forman: 'No prospect of my book going ahead just at the present, though I have just as much faith in its central idea and the light thrown by it on many things in life and literature, yet I see great difficulty in carrying it out logically to its ultimate conclusion. Still I hope some day to get at least a skeleton of it set down in black and white. I have been thinking of putting a sketch of it in a series of Magazine articles. But I do not know what I shall do. I am a good deal in the dumps lately.'[22]

Bucke eventually adopted the latter plan, and his ideas appeared in two articles, 'The Functions of the Great Sympathetic Nervous System' and 'The Moral Nature and the Great Sympathetic', in the *American Journal of Insanity* in 1877 and 1878.[23] Although Bucke returned to the practice of medicine in 1874, after his venture into land speculation, he did not intend to stay in Sarnia. He hoped to be appointed head of a new asylum for the insane in Hamilton, Ontario, did receive the appointment, and moved to Hamilton in March 1876.[24] He remained in Hamilton, however, only for a few months. On the death in February 1877 of the medical superintendent of the Asylum for the Insane in London, Ontario, Bucke was promoted to this position. He remained in London for the rest of his professional life.

2

'An average man magnified to the dimensions of a god'

Bucke first met Whitman on Thursday, 18 October 1877, while he was on a two-week business trip to Boston, New York, and Philadelphia. In 'Memories of Walt Whitman' of 1894 he recalls that he made the visit uninvited: 'I wrote to Walt Whitman that I had read his books, thought very highly of them, was anxious to see the author, and proposed to call upon him. Of course (I knew afterwards it was "of course," though not by any means at that time)—of course I received no answer. However, I wished to see, and meant to see, the poet, so— without having heard from him—one day about noon I crossed the Delaware to make my experimental call.'[1] (An account of this visit is found in Bucke's letters to his wife and to Harry Forman [letters 2–3].)

In subsequent writings Bucke frequently referred to this first meeting, stressing its lasting consequences. Six years later, in his biography of Whitman, he included the incident but disguised his own role, perhaps in order to be more objective:

> The following is the experience of a person well known to the present writer. He called on Walt Whitman and spent an hour at his home in Camden, in the autumn of 1877. He had never seen the poet before, but he had been profoundly reading his works for some years. He said that Walt Whitman only spoke to him about a hundred words altogether, and these quite ordinary and commonplace; that he did not realize anything peculiar while with him, but shortly after leaving a state of mental exaltation set in, which he could only describe by comparing to slight intoxication by champagne, or to falling in love! And this exaltation, he said, lasted at least six weeks in a clearly marked degree, so that, for at least that length of time, he was plainly different from his ordinary self. Neither, he said, did it then, or since pass away, though it ceased to be felt as something new and strange, but became a permanent element in his life, a strong and living force (as he described it), making for purity and happiness. I may add that this person's whole life has been changed by that contact (no doubt the previous reading of *Leaves of Grass* also), his temper, character, entire spiritual being, outer life, conversation etc. elevated and purified in an extraordinary degree. He tells me that at first he used often to speak to friends and acquaintances of his feeling for Walt Whitman and the *Leaves*, but after a time he found that he could not make himself understood, and that some even thought his mental balance impaired. He gradually learned to keep silence upon the subject, but the feeling did not abate, nor its influence upon his life grow less.[2]

Twenty years later, in his preface to an edition of Whitman's letters to his friend Peter Doyle, *Calamus*, Bucke again referred to the meeting, pointing out the difficulty of communicating the vast significance of such an apparently ordinary encounter: 'Any attempt to convey to another even the faintest notion of the effect upon me of that short and seemingly commonplace interview would be certainly hopeless, probably foolish. Briefly, it would be nothing more than the simple truth to state that I was, by it, lifted to and set upon a higher plane of existence, upon which I have more or less consciously lived ever since'.[3] The most complete analysis of this meeting, however, is found in his paper 'Memories of Walt Whitman'. After nearly twenty years, crossing the Delaware, he said, had become for him a symbol and proof of an afterlife:

> When I think how many dozens of times, all seasons, for fifteen years, I afterwards crossed the same river, with the same purpose—to hold that hand, to look at that face and to listen to that noble and musical voice—and that now that is all over and past, forever gone. When I think of these things, I sometimes feel as if I should die outright, and end the matter, but that far down in me, somewhere, below clear consciousness, below thought, almost below feeling, there is something that, speaking with absolute conviction, with supreme mastery over all the so called facts of science and experience, tells me that when the right time comes I shall cross another Delaware and land at another City and that then there I shall take the same hand, look into the same eyes and listen once more to the same voice.[4]

Before a gathering of fellow Whitmanites, Bucke answers the indirect invitation Whitman issued in 'Crossing Brooklyn Ferry': 'And you that shall cross from shore to shore years hence are more to me, and more in my meditations, than you might suppose.'

It is unfortunate that so few letters between Bucke and Whitman survive to document the initial stage of Bucke's discipleship. In the period from his first visit to Whitman in the fall of 1877 to Whitman's visit to Canada in the summer of 1880, there are only six extant letters from Bucke to Whitman and two from Whitman to Bucke, but the letters from Bucke to his wife and those between Bucke and Harry Buxton Forman help to fill in the picture (letters 2–7).

During this period Bucke's relations with Whitman were both personal and public. Through letters, visits, an offer to lend money, and a standing invitation to visit him in London, Bucke developed a degree of intimacy with Whitman. At this time Bucke also began proselytizing for Whitman in print, in speeches, in editions of Whitman's work.

It is easy to find fault with the method and content of *Man's Moral Nature*. Bucke forges ahead with the fierce energy of a self-educated man, borrowing from physiology, biology, anthropology, philosophy, theology, history, literature, personal observations, and the philosophic utterances of his friends. On the surface, it appears to be a philosophic treatise, directed to an audience of non-specialists, in which the author ranges over many areas of knowledge to develop, illustrate, and prove his thesis. His method appears to be inductive; that is, by carefully examining the nature and function of the sympathetic nervous system, he will establish the origin, operation, and evolution of man's moral nature. Having demonstrated the evolution of this nature, he can then prophesy for man a future in which all things are getting better and better faster and faster.

As a philosophic treatise based on the inductive method, the book is unconvincing on the popular level and inept on the serious level. It is really an attempt at metaphor, rather than an attempt to establish a philosophic system. Bucke was a mystic: at the age of thirty-five, he experienced a vision of the nature of the universe and man's relation to it. From that day on, he devoted his life to finding evidence for what he knew in his heart to be true, proceeding from illumination to example. Unfortunately, he was no poet: he did not find an objective correlative for his illumination but tried to demonstrate and justify it to others by means of an unwieldy philosophic structure. Bucke's vision is the cement that holds his system together; without it, we are left with a heap of outdated examples.

In a letter to Harry Buxton Forman of 27 November 1878, Bucke revealed the genesis of the book:

I think it is somewhat remarkable from the first moment that the central idea flashed across my mind going home from the P. O. that night in the spring of 1871 till now. I have never had to alter a thought that has gone into it, and although I did not see all its parts that first night the whole book was revealed to me then, the subsequent process has consisted in [sic] unfolding and formulating of this idea, no doubt of the truth of this idea or of its parts has ever troubled me though as a general thing I am not given to too much fixity of opinion.[5]

Bucke's grand synthesis was based on two concepts: the scope and physiological foundation of man's moral nature, and the all-pervasive force of evolution. One must realize that he uses the word 'moral' in a peculiar way—one should substitute 'emotional' to follow his reasoning. According to Bucke, man's moral nature may be divided into three parts: his 'active nature', with which he performs the acts he is capable of; his 'intellectual nature', with which he knows, and his 'moral nature', with which he feels. All that we feel may be reduced to positive and negative functions. The positive functions are love and faith (faith in the sense of trust), and the negative functions are hate and fear. Everything we feel is made up of these four elements, either separately or in combination with other elements of the moral or intellectual nature. Through the positive functions of our moral nature we feel beauty and goodness; through the negative ones we feel ugliness and evil. Man's intellectual nature has its biological foundation in the cerebrospinal system; his moral nature has its foundation in the sympathetic nervous system. As man developed, his positive moral functions (love and faith) came to be stronger than his negative moral functions (fear and hate). From this we may assume, says Bucke, that there has been a continuous evolution in man's moral nature, reflecting a development of his sympathetic nervous system. The object of the development of all internal functions is to bring man closer to the true nature of the universe. Just as we now know more about the world than the savages did, so, too, we feel more accurately about the world. And since we feel more love and faith than hate and fear, it follows that the world is a place of beauty and goodness, rather than ugliness and evil.

This summary does not do justice to the complexity and range of Bucke's methods. Perhaps an example of his logic may illustrate his methodology. One of the eight proofs he adduces for the physical basis of man's moral nature is the longevity of the Jews. Happy people (those whose moral nature is highly developed), he says, live longer than sad people (those whose moral nature is relatively undeveloped). Since length of life is determined to a large extent by the functions of the sympathetic nervous system, which controls such internal activities as digestion and the secretions of various glands, it follows that the moral nature must also have its basis in this system. Bucke notes:

> I estimate that the average life of the Jew is at least six or eight years longer than the average life of the non-Jewish inhabitants of the various countries in which the Jews live. . . . The Jews, then, have an extraordinary amount of vitality . . . [because] they lead a more moral life than other people. . . . Well, then, supposing that Jews' lives are better than our lives, it is a fair inference that their moral natures are, on an average, better, that is, higher than our moral natures—that with them love and faith are more developed, and hate and fear more restricted in proportion than with us. But although these considerations are entitled to a certain amount of weight, I do not propose to rest my argument on them. I have surer ground. This ground is that the Jews have initiated the most advanced religions of the world during the whole course of its history. . . . Here, then, we have one instance of length of life associated with a high moral nature.[6]

Bucke is now able to classify and evaluate human accomplishments. Achievements in philosophy and science issue from man's intellectual nature; achievements in art and religion issue from his moral nature. Religion is the expression of faith, and art is the expression of love. This designation of religion and art as expressions of the moral nature is both descriptive and prescriptive, that is, only their moral elements are essential:

> The moral nature of all men, however, possesses this quality—that it can be acted upon, moved, elevated, and there is a mysterious relation, a sympathy, existing among men by which we are all compelled, in spite of ourselves, to seek to impress our influence, whether for good or evil, upon one another. Under the operation of this law, the men of superior moral natures have sought for and found various means by which they might convey to others their moral attitude toward themselves and their surroundings. These means we call by the generic name of art (p. 170).

In religion, the intellectual content, that is, the doctrine, is simply a tool for expressing faith: 'the intellectual conceptions by which faith toward the unknown is interpreted are purely factitious—are useful and truthful solely as an interpretation of faith, and have no objective value at all . . . ' (pp. 181–82). In art poets who emphasize reason are of the second rank: 'This class of poets is often greatly admired by their contemporaries, but they make no impression upon the great heart of humanity, and their works soon die' (p. 172). Similarly, in religion 'The moral nature is undoubtedly influenced by the perusal of books, but not, or not much, by the ideas contained in them. We must always recollect that, in almost every book . . . we come into contact in reading it with the moral nature of the writer as well as with his intellectual nature, and it is this moral contact which influences our moral nature, and not the intellectual contact' (pp. 184–85).

By situating the moral nature in the sympathetic nervous system Bucke has made the 'gut-response' quite literally the final criterion of authenticity in both religion and art. It is the body which is the judge in these matters, and it judges by feeling: the more faith we feel, the greater the religion which stimulates it; the more love we feel, the greater the work of art.

As an example of the inadequacy of the intellect in matters concerned with the moral nature, Bucke points to the failure of the Jews to accept Christ. One of the reasons why they failed to accept a man in whom 'faith reached a level which it had never touched before in any human being' (p. 181) was that their moral natures were too intensely bound up with their intellectual natures: in brief, they were unwilling to discard their doctrines in order to appreciate and embrace the great advance in faith represented by Christ. Bucke offers this example to his contemporaries as both a warning and a prophecy:

> only one Jew [Paul], as far as we know, who appears to have held the religious convictions of his age and country with the usual firmness of the cultivated Jew, was converted to Christianity, and this conversion, we are told, required a miracle to effect it. So, too, in what would be a parallel though not such an extreme case, it may be strongly suspected that, should a man appear to-day with a moral nature bearing the same relation to that of the ordinary orthodox Christian which the moral nature of Jesus bore to that of the ordinary orthodox Jew, he would make no converts among orthodox Christians. They would reject him almost as indignantly as the Jews rejected Jesus (pp. 182–83).

Because the advance in art and religion has been quantitative, says Bucke, we may not assume that any absolutes have been reached. Christ did not proclaim once and for all the true and full nature of faith; he was merely one, albeit the loftiest, in a series of innovators in religion (p. 183).

The concluding chapter of *Man's Moral Nature*, 'The Inference To Be Drawn from the Development of the Moral Nature as to the Essential Fact of the Universe', is more a hymn to progress than an inference, despite its title. Bucke points out the extent of the advance in man's active and intellectual natures and the function of this advance. Through his active nature, he has mastered such forces as steam and electricity; through his intellectual nature, he has come to understand many of the laws of the universe. The ultimate function of these advances has been to bring man closer to things as they really are. Bucke then proposes that these advances in the active and intellectual nature must, of course, have counterparts in the moral nature. The abatement of fear and hate and the development of faith and love are analogues to man's growth in power and knowledge, and there is room for infinite development and expansion in all three areas.

In his rapturous conclusion, Bucke, perhaps unwittingly, reveals the real nature of his work. He justifies his infinite optimism by pointing out that what he has revealed is instinctively known by everyone to be true: 'Infinite faith and love are justified. That means that there is nothing to warrant fear and nothing to warrant hate in the universe. . . . This is no new theory. We all recognize, and have recognized all along, that this is so, that the highest moral nature is nearest in accord with the truth of things' (pp. 199–200). After devoting his entire volume to proving his thesis through reason, Bucke finally adopts Whitman's rhetorical stance: 'To elaborate is no avail, learn'd and unlearn'd feel that it is so.' But Whitman stated his position early in 'Song of Myself' (l. 47) and proceeded to reiterate what he knew without attempting to find proofs. Bucke, unfortunately, set out to *prove* what he knew, and after offering laborious and, at times, incredible proofs concluded that the best proof was no proof since everyone 'recognize[s] all along, that this is so'.

Both Whitman and Bucke end in the same place. Whitman, however, phrases his conclusion as an observation: 'Do you see O my brothers and sisters? / It is not chaos or death—it is form, union, plan—it is eternal life—it is Happiness' ('Song of Myself', ll. 1317–19). Bucke's is an injunction:

> We see, then, do we not, that religion, morality, and happiness are three names for the same thing—moral elevation.
>
> This, then, is the end, the conclusion of the whole matter: Love all things—not because it is your duty to do so, but because all things are worthy of your love. Hate nothing. Fear nothing. Have

absolute faith. Whoso will do this is wise; he is more than wise—
he is happy (p. 200).

The presence of Walt Whitman is implicit throughout
Man's Moral Nature. Two quotations from his work serve as
epigraphs for the fifth and sixth chapters, and the work is
dedicated to him. The epigraph to the fifth chapter—'The
Lord advances, and yet advances; / Always the shadow in
front; always the reaching hand, bringing up the laggards'
('Faces', ll. 46–47)—points to the irresistible force of evolution; the epigraph to the sixth chapter—'I swear the earth
shall surely be complete to him or her who shall be complete! / I swear the earth remains jagged and broken only to
him or her who remains jagged and broken!' ('Song of the
Rolling Earth', ll. 89–90)—points to the correspondence between perfection within and perfection without. But the
importance of Whitman for Bucke is far more than the-
matic: Whitman is the living proof of Bucke's evolutionary
hypothesis. If man's moral nature is indeed evolving, then
Bucke must offer some supreme example of contemporary
faith or love. (It is important to note that at this stage Bucke
has not as yet explicitly united the two elements of love
and faith in Whitman, making him the supreme poet-
priest.) The very fact that Whitman is neglected by his
contemporaries, like Christ, seems to strengthen Bucke's
case.

But only in the dedication is Whitman specifically mentioned, and in terms of literary effect a dedication is more
in the nature of a rhetorical flourish than a convincing
proof: 'I dedicate this book to the man who inspired it—to
the man who of all men past and present that I have known
has the most exalted moral nature—to WALT WHITMAN'
(p. v). As Bucke himself realized, *Man's Moral Nature* was
the theoretical introduction to a biography of Whitman and
to a criticism of his poems.

It is difficult to determine Whitman's response to *Man's
Moral Nature* because all the letters from Whitman to Bucke

in this period appear to be lost. Whitman did not mention the book to anyone else in his letters, and when Bucke attempted to develop its ideas further in the manuscript of his biography of Whitman, the poet deleted such passages.

Perhaps the best description of Bucke's intellectual procedures is provided by Edward Carpenter, in discussing the influence of illumination on *Leaves of Grass*. Carpenter mentions those who neither recover from the experience nor succeed in expressing it:

> many people of mystical tendency, after a momentary illumination of the kind, relapse into a sort of drivel for the rest of their natural lives—circling always round something which they have neither clearly apprehended nor can conclusively forget—but out of the memory of which they hatch systems and "revelations" and dogmas without end. And indeed, if we suppose, with Dr. Bucke, that the faculty is one that is gradually evolving in human nature, there can be nothing more likely than that its first exercise should be accompanied by much doubt and illusion and disturbance of the intelligence generally, and even of the moral nature.[7]

21 April 1895

My dear Horace

I have a card from Carpenter: He
says: "I am anxious that L. of G. should
"be published in England at a reasonable
"price — say 3/6 or 5/. It is high time
"this were done. Are any negotiations pending
"on the Subject, or can I do anything to
"push it on? If you have time I wish
"you would consider the matter seriously."

Shall write (this day) to Hamed on
the matter — I wish you would meet and
consult — I feel strongly that Carpenter is
right and that it is our manifest duty to
arouse and move at once in this matter.

42

I am also strongly of the opinion that
we should take steps looking to a cheap
Ed. of the Leaves in america

I am dear Horace

Faithfully Yours
RM Bucke

(1)

To Walt Whitman

Sarnia,
December 19. 1870.

Walt Whitman,

Dear Sir: Will you please send to the enclosed address
two copies of "Leaves of Grass", *one* copy of "Passage to
India" and *one* copy of "Democratic Vistas". Enclosed you
will find $7.25—$6.75 for the books and $0.50 for postage. I
do not know exactly what this last item will be but I fancy
$0.50 will be enough to pay for it. [—] I am an old reader of
your works, and a very great admirer of them. About two
years ago I borrowed a copy of the 1855 edition of "Leaves
of Grass" and I have a great ambition to own a copy of this
edition myself; would it be possible to get one? Before
getting that the only thing I had ever seen of yours was

43

Rossetti's selection. Lately I have got a copy of the 1867 edition of "Leaves of Grass" and I have compared the "Walt Whitman" in that with the same poem in the 1855 edition and I must say I like the earlier edition best.

I have an idea I shall be in Washington in the course of 1871; if I am it would give me much pleasure to see you, if you would not object, I am afraid, however, that, like other celebrities, you have more people call upon you than you care about seeing; in that case I should not wish to annoy you—At all events

Believe me
Faithfully yours,
R. M. Bucke—[1]

Address
D[r] R. Maurice Bucke
Sarnia
Ontario
Canada

---

[1]Whitman presented this letter to Traubel on 16 July 1888 with the following comment: 'This is already a letter of long ago: this was Bucke's first appearance on the scene. You will notice, he comes in quite frankly, quite frankly, without flattering adjectives, yet also without impudence. To Bucke, to me, the document is historic. Read it aloud to me: I would like to hear it again before you take it away.' After Traubel had read the letter, Whitman remarked: 'Try to think what that innocent letter has led on to—what it was frankly to mean to Maurice, what it has long meant, means today, to me—and to you, too, Horace, God help you: for we are all aboard the same ship—be it frail or strong, aboard the same ship' (Traubel, II, 6–7).

(2)

To Jessie Bucke

Continental Hotel—Phil[a]
Thursday [October] 18th 1877

My darling

I have had bad luck getting letters from you. I got one at New York & one at Boston and I made sure I should find one here on my arrival last night—but no—Nary letter.

I expect I shall leave here some time tomorrow though it is just possible I may leave tonight—This will depend on how I get on with the hospitals—I called this morning upon Walt Whitman and we were old friends at once. He is the most delightfull man I ever saw—

I stayed over an hour at his house and then we crossed the river to Phil[a] together [/] He made a kind of half promise that he would come and see us some time at London and spend some days—I would give anything that he would—his health has been very poor for years but it is now slowly mending

‑He has an invitation at present to go to California on a trip but he has not quite made up his mind whether or not to accept it—

I think I shall certainly be home on Saturday

I am always my sweet darling your loving husband

R. M. Bucke

(3)

To Harry Buxton Forman

London, Ont. October 24, '77

My dear Harry

We have written to one another so seldom lately and I have been so occupied with my work that I really forget how our correspondence stands. It seems to me that you owe me a letter but I am not quite sure about it. I know I have a lot of things to write about but I am not at all sure that I can recollect all of them. In the first place I have got all of your Shelley and it is a magnificent book.[1] I understand that the Athenaeum "went for you a little"—thought you had no business to restore "Laon and Cynthia"[2] or some such nonsense. I see Russel Reynolds Vol. IV is out at last.[3] How about books ordered through you, if you hold any money of mine in your hands lay it out as soon as convenient on books which I have given you names of. If you have no money of mine buy no books for me. If I am in your debt let me know and I will pay up. There is no sense in my sending to you for books now I can get them nearly as cheap from Toronto and give no one any trouble. Besides I am apt to order the same book twice when I order them at more than one place so we will close our accounts and quit the book business. The pictures of yours which were unsold when I wrote about the pictures last remain unsold.[4] I thought they were all going to be taken in Sarnia and not one of them was taken. I have them now at a picture dealers in London and I dare say that he will get them off after a while. I have just returned from a two weeks trip in the Eastern States. I was in Boston, New York and Philadelphia. When I was in the latter city I crossed the Delaware River to Camden, New Jersey and went to see Walt Whitman. We were old friends in less than two minutes and I spent a good part of the forenoon with him. We then crossed the river together to Philadelphia as he had an engagement there. I hardly know how to tell you about W. W. If I tried to say how he impressed me you would probably put it down to exaggeration. I have never seen any man to compare with him—any man the least like him—he seems more than a man and yet in all his looks and ways entirely commonplace ("Do I contradict myself"?) He is an average man magnified to the dimensions of a god—but this does not give you the least idea of what he is like and I despair of giving you any idea at all however slight—I may say that I experienced what I have heard so much about the extraordinary magnetism of his presence—I not only felt deeply in an indescribable way towards him—but I think that that short interview has altered the attitude of my moral nature to everything—I feel differently, I feel more than I did before—this may be fancy but I do not think it is—I saw some thing of this same quality of Walt's objectively as well as subjectively during the few minutes that we were on the street together. We met a boy and a man who knew Walt—He said to the boy "Well Atty is that you?" hardly above his breath—without smiling, scarcely

46

glancing at him. The boy's face reddened and lit up as I think I never saw a face—the man was a rough, dirty, dark chap—as common and common-place a man as you could find—Walt hardly looked at him and said quietly "Good day Bill"—the man smiled, his face reddened—he became transfigured instantly—there was no mistaking the affection he felt—In conversation Walt expressed no opinions—he does not praise, he never smiles—he has no trace of wit—his talk is not intellectual—but you think you could listen to it forever—but it is no use for me to try to give any idea of the man because I have no idea of him myself—I cant grasp him, I cannot take him in—he is immense—the best of it is that he half promised to come and see me in London next summer and stay awhile. I would rather Walt would make me this visit than that I should receive a large legacy. Walt was dressed in such clothes as the better class of laborers and mechanics wear in this country. He wore a coarse cotton shirt open at the neck—a checkered blue and white cotton neckerchief and gray woolen clothes—all his clothes had evidently seen a good deal of wear but they were absolutely clean. I dont think I ever saw another man who looked so *clean* as Walt did. His hair is very gray and rather thin about the top and front of his head—he wears it long—his beard is long and grey of course he wears it all—I dont think he ever shaved any part of his face—for some years his breath has not been good. He had some form of partial paralysis which is slowly passing off. He still walks with some little difficulty, uses a cane and takes the arm of whoever he is with—The house he lives in is his brother's house, he pays his board there, he is very comfortable—he says they are very kind to him—I can easily believe that. The house is new brick—good sized, well furnished, a very comfortable house indeed to all appearance—but I must quit Walt for I have other things to write about.

I expect every day now to receive the Journal with my essay in it.[5] I shall not go on with the publication of it at present—that is I shall not publish it in book form as it is now. I am getting a few extra copies and shall send you one which will have to answer for both you and Alfred.

I am getting on slowly with the book.[6] I have great confidence that I shall be able to make something of it. The book may be ready for publication by this time next year or perhaps not for two years.

When does your edition of Shelley's Prose come out? Will it be in vols. like the Poetry, and how many vols. will it make?[7] If there are any extra good copies struck off, I want one to match the poetry.

What is Alfred doing since he got through with Wagner?[8] He worries himself too much, that fellow. It would be far better for him if he took things a little easier and wrote to his friends a little oftener and a little longer letters—he owes me a long letter which he always promises and never pays. Tell him I read a long article on Schopenhauer in the "Revue des deux Mondes" the other day and that at the present time I don't think much of *that* philosopher.

You must send this letter to Alfred and let him see about Walt for I want him to write another account for him. I am very busy just now since my return from the States.

Is there anything in the literary world? I hear that Swinburne is writing a novel? Is he? And if so is it a good one and what is the name of it? I do not ask about Browning any more. They are played out. Do you know a poet named Payne?[9] What has he written and what merit has it? I had a blasted Englishman here the other day who thought the said Payne was a great poet. I suppose though it is all humbug.

Give my best regards to Mrs. Forman.

Write sometimes,
Affectionately yours,
R. M. Bucke

---

[1]The fourth and final volume of *The Poetical Works of Percy Bysshe Shelley*, ed. Harry Buxton Forman, 4 vols. (London, 1876–77).
[2]The original title of Shelley's *The Revolt of Islam* was *Laon and Cantha*.

[3]Sir John Russell Reynolds, *A System of Medicine*, 5 vols. (London, 1866–79).
[4]In March Bucke suggested to Forman that he lend him some of his engravings in the hope that his friends who saw them might buy a few (letter of 30 March 1877, Seaborn typescript).
[5]'The Function of the Great Sympathetic Nervous System', *American Journal of Insanity*, 34 (October 1877), 115–59.
[6]*Man's Moral Nature*.
[7]The edition, in eight volumes, was published in London over a five-year period, from 1876 to 1880.
[8]*Wagner Festival . . . 1877. Selections from the German Text of Der Ring Des Nibelungen, Tannhäuser, Der fliegende Holländer, Lohengrin, Die Meistersinger, etc. With English Versions by . . . A. Forman* (1877).
[9]*Poems*, by James Payn, the English novelist and editor of *Chamber's Journal* and *The Cornhill Magazine*, appeared in 1853.

(4)

To Walt Whitman

Nov. 4 1877

My dear Walt Whitman

I send you by this mail a copy of one essay of mine[1] which is just published—I do not know whether it will be of any interest to you—it ought to be for it was inspired directly by yourself—it is part of a book which I have been engaged upon for about six years—the book is on "Man's Moral Nature." this book as I say was inspired by yourself about six years ago in the city of London England.[2]

This is a payment of that truth which is said to be stranger than fiction.

I hope to publish the book in a year or at most two from this time and I intend if you do not object to dedicate it to you. This letter has rather a mysterious air about it especially as being written by a "materialist" to a "materialist"[3] [/] Some day if ever we meet again as I trust we shall I will explain it.

I am always

Affectionately yours
R. M. Bucke

[1]'The Function of the Great Sympathetic Nervous System'.
[2]During the illumination in the spring of 1872.

49

³Bucke's philosophical materialism is clearly expressed in his epigraph from Comte: 'Les regions speculative et active du cerveau n'ont de communications nerveuses qu'avec les sens et les muscles pour aperçevoir et modifier le monde exterieur' (*Man's Moral Nature*, p. 2). The application of the term to Whitman is less clear, however.

(5)

To Jessie Bucke

Philadelphia
May 12 [1878]
Sunday

My darling

I reached here about half past four yesterday afternoon—I had to wait about two hours in New York for a train to this city but with that exception I travelled all the time—I didn't get a very good sleep somehow or other and last night I was pretty tired but I feel first class this morning—I saw Walt yesterday evening for a couple of hours and I shall not see him any more as he has an appointment to spend the day today in the country—I asked him when he was coming to see us and I told him that you had sent him your love and that you wanted him to come to London—He has promised to come towards the end of June—I am to go to Niagara to meet him—Walt will stay with us some weeks, perhaps a month; he is not very well and he had some doubts about the prudence of undertaking so long a journey but I persuaded him that it could not do him any harm and would probably do him good—I told him that he would have a comfortable room to himself and that he could stay by himself as much as he chose—he still seemed doubtfull about coming untill I told him that you had sent him your love and that you were very anxious he should come—this decided him & he said he would come. You will not be able to help liking him for old and broken down as he is by age and illness he is still a most magnificent man—and rough as he may look to you at first he has perhaps the warmest heart that ever beat on this earth—I look forwards to his visit with

50

great pleasure and not only so but I consider it a very great priveledge for the children that they may be able to say in after life that they have seen Walt Whitman—besides all this I owe Walt Whitman a larger debt of gratitude—and I am anxious to do something w̄h may be some return to him however slight for what he has done for me—You too my best darling owe him more than you know.—When I come home I shall get you, if you will to write him a little note to enclose in one of my letters to him. I leave here tomorrow noon and reach Washing about 4 o'clock—I shall write to you from there in a couple of days—

Goodly my sweet—I love you more than you know or can think. Kiss the dear children for me

I am always

Yours only
R. M. Bucke

(6)

To Harry Buxton Forman

Phila, Penn
Sunday
May 12th
1878

Ansd: 16/6/78

Promising to write from Marlow about Walt.

My dear Harry:

I reached here last night on my way to Washington. I have seen Walt Whitman again and have spent a couple of hours with him. I gave him your message and he said that he would hunt a MSS for you and send it. I am to give him your address for this end and you may expect to hear from him before many weeks. It is likely he will send you some of his hair at the same time. He seemed pleased with his message and was not altogether unfamiliar with your name, as to my surprise, he had heard of your ed. of Shelley. He had a vague idea that he had heard from you and [I] have told him I am almost sure he is mistaken. I was pretty sure you had never had any direct communication with him. He says that he gets more orders for his books from England than he does from this country. He has not been as well for a couple of months back as he was before that and he was not in good spirits. I believe that he feels the neglect of the world more than he cares to admit, and how can he fail to feel it? He has given the world his time, his labor, his love, himself, and now he is ill and old and the world will hardly give him bread to eat. It is hard case of ingratitude. Walt has promised to come to London about the 20th or 25th of June and pay me a visit of some weeks, I hope I shall be able to cheer him up and do him good. I talked to him about an English ed. of his works either entire or the poems in one vol. I thought it ought to succeed and I believe that if there were good publishers who would undertake it—it would succeed. I said I would write to you on the subject and consult you on the question. Of course if it is done it must be without castration. Walt would hardly submit to this and I would not care to have anything to do with such an enterprise as would entail this sacrifice. For my part I have not patience to argue of the purity of Walt's books. I told Walt that I thought it would aid the success of the enterprise if a short life of himself were added to the work. I do not think he would object to this and would consent perhaps to supply some material for said life. I would like to write such a life myself if I saw my way to it—but I don't. I doubt if I could do it; my feelings would be too much implicated and my knowledge would come short I am afraid of material for a full and true portrait. But give your ideas about the publication whether it would be likely to pay—and if these questions can be answered in the affirmative—what you think about the details, about life, or whether the whole works should be published in two volumes,—or the poems in one volume. I will tell you what I could do, and I believe I would do it better than any man living, or rather I believe I am the only man living who could do it. I could write an essay on the poems giving some idea of their scope and meaning, of their place in literature, and of their value. This might be done as a review of the book and if a good magazine could be got to publish it, it might help the sale. I need not pursue the subject now till I hear something from you on the matter. I leave here in the morning for Washington where I shall be most of the week. I think I shall then go to Montreal, Ottawa, and pay a visit to Jack Harkness.[1]

I expect that Eustace[2] sailed yesterday from Quebec. I wrote to him some days ago from London to tell him to call on you for the books in London, or to write you word where to send them and when to send them that he might get them to bring out with him. I wrote you last week ago winding up the picture matter in a sort of a way and sending you a trifle of money to go on with the purchase of books I want. I trust that you will get this letter and that you will find it satisfactory. I hope you will be able to get the books I want. You will be disgusted, my dear fellow, that I can not come to England after all but such is life.

Please give my best regards to Mrs. Forman

I am always yours affectionately,

R. M. Bucke

[1]Dr. Harkness was a classmate of Bucke's and one of his closest friends.
[2]Bucke's brother, Philip Eustace.

(7)

To Harry Buxton Forman

London, Dec. 23d, 1878

My dear Harry:

Your letter of Dec. 23d and 25th followed me from here to New York, then back home again, then to Sarnia and caught me at the first named place this morning just as I was leaving for London. Before this you will have got mine of Dec. 4th and will know that the book is done.[1] I cannot tell you what a relief it is to me to have it off my mind. I did not at all know what weight I was carrying until I got rid of it. Well I took the MSS to New York, went to MacMillan and Co., agent there and found he did not publish, was a mere agent for a London house,—went to Appleton & Co., they did not want the MSS at any price, would not publish it, would not look at it,—went to Scribner & Co., do, do, do. Went to Henry Holt and Company, found young Holt in, said he would send for MSS and have it read. He sent for it but it was returned the next day, evidently unlooked at, a circular sent with it to say "it was not suited for their purpose." Then I began to get mad. However, before damning the whole race of publishers I made one more trial, viz. Putnam & Co. Saw Putnam himself had quite a talk with him. He promised to have the MSS read and to read it himself, so I left it with him and expect to hear in a couple of weeks what he proposes to do about it. Should he decline to publish it I shall try Hind and Houghton of Boston and if I fail with them I shall send the MSS to you and try and get me a publisher in London. If I fail there I shall have it published by Willing & Williamson of Toronto or get some man to print it and publish it myself. But damn the impudence of these American publishers I say. You see that they steal all the books they want from the English and Continental writers and get the books of known men in this way and so do not want to publish the work of a man unknown to the public, no odds how good it is, in every instance I offered to guarantee all expenses but that did not make any difference; they said they did not mind the expense but that they want to publish books that would pay and they said that a book called "Man's Moral Nature" would not pay, no odds how able it was. I assured them that it would pay but they absolutely insisted that they knew better. I should not have dared to ask you to edit the book in England for I know that you have more work on your hands than you can well do but I assure you my dear fellow that I am most grateful for your offer and shall at least partly accept it if I have to send the MSS to England and if I get a publisher there, I shall want however to correct the proofs once myself. I am in hopes though that if Putnam really has the MSS read and especially if he reads it himself that he will publish it. In that case I shall make arrangements through him to send sheets to England, say to MacMilland & Co., and publish the book simultaneously in London and N.Y. as at first intended, however, more about this again. I may say that my faith in the book does not fail one iota, and in fact never has since the first day it was conceived eight years ago. I am delighted my dear Harry that your little girl is better. I cannot imagine that there can be very great cause for uneasiness about her now, I have very little doubt that she will continue to do well. I am glad you are working at Shelley's prose. I shall be very glad to get it when it comes out, do not work too hard, that is a good fellow. Keep Walt's letter by all means. I am likely to have plenty of them for Walt and I are now quite friends. When Jessie and I were East we went to Philadelphia on purpose to see him and he spent the afternoon and evening at the hotel with us. He is undoubtedly the most delightful man in the world; Jessie used to laugh at me for going on so about him but now she likes him as much as I do and I expect to innoculate her with his poetry before very long. He has promised to make us a long visit of a month or more next summer "as sure as death and taxes." I expect he will come about 1st June next. He sent a long message to you which I have in my note book at the house and which I will copy before I finish this letter. I am glad to hear that "Leaves of Grass" sells in London. I doubt it does not sell very well on this side and I must say it seems to me a bad sign for the American people that it does not. But you know "The proof of a poet shall be sternly deferred until his country absorb him as affectionately as he has absorbed it," and "I am willing to wait to be understood by the path of the— [*sic*] of myself". I have received all the books you mentioned as I think you will see by my last, as soon as I owe you something (as I think I do now) send my bill and I will send some money to cover it and much ahead or little, I have Vol. 4 of Russell Reynold's Medicine. I got it in Toronto. You had better send me volume 5 as soon as it comes out. I will recollect not to order it here. I think it is a good idea Mrs. Forman and Jessie coming to live with you. As you say it will throw Alfred and you more together which will be pleasant and profitable for both of you. I am very sorry to hear Alfred's financial outlook is cloudy. I trust it will clear off. If any of Alfred's translations are published of course I want a copy at once. I should very much like to see any of them. His *"Ring des Nibelungs"* I did not care for the subject. I fancied you must have the music with it to appreciate it, not that I should appreciate Wagner's music. Our photos are now out and I shall order some more and send you a set. I do not really know how you were missed out before. You ought to have had a set last summer. I have given up the notion of the likeness of the author of my book at the present and the cuts of the Nervous Systems. I can have them done here if the book is published here. No great art will be required for them.

December 24th, 1878

This is Walt's message to you: "Give my regards to Mr. Forman and tell him that I have nothing definite to say at the present about an English ed. of my poems, but I will keep it in mind and will keep him in mind in connection with it. Perhaps next summer I shall have something definite to say about it. Just now I do not think anything can be done. Tell him also that [what] I have to say about the English Ed. will be first presented to him. I have many friends in England but he will be the first consulted."

I don't know that I have anything to add to this letter my dear Harry except to ask you to send me a copy of Augusta Webster's poems. I want to see them myself and then send them to Walt who saw them once for a short time and wants to see them again.

Good-bye dear fellow. I shall write you again when there is anything further to tell about the book.

I am always your friend

R. M. Bucke

Give my love to Mrs. H. B. F.—Mrs. Forman, Jessie and Alfred.

---

[1]*Man's Moral Nature.*

'You are the terrible surgeon with the knife & saw'

In the summer of 1880 Whitman finally paid the visit Bucke had been hoping for since 1877. Bucke accompanied Whitman from Camden to London, Ontario, where they arrived on 4 June. Both London newspapers published interviews with the poet the next day. Bucke had delivered a lecture in London on 27 February which sparked some public discussion concerning Whitman's religious orthodoxy, and to pacify the Londoners either Bucke or Whitman himself supplied the reporter from the *Advertiser* with a copy of the poet's *Memoranda during the War* (1875). The interview includes an ex-

cerpt from Whitman's diary, dated 22 July 1863. After describing how the poet read from the Evangelists to Oscar, a
dying soldier, the excerpt closes: 'I read slowly, for Oscar
was feeble. It pleased him very much, yet the tears were in
his eyes, and he asked me if I enjoyed religion. I said,
"Perhaps not, my dear, in the way you mean, and yet
maybe it is the same thing.' " The reporter from the *Advertiser* concluded that Whitman was a respectable man: 'The
hour was late and it was not well that the fatigue of the
journey should be supplemented by too much conversation, yet it was learned that Walt Whitman is a man with
whom any can converse, with distinct convictions on literature and religion, and while it is not the province of the
reporter to pronounce upon his orthodoxy, there can be no
doubt that he is a reverent man with no suggestion of
irreverence or pruriency in his talk'.[1] It may, I think, be
assumed that Bucke, perhaps with the cooperation of Whitman, arranged for these interviews. Whitman, in turn, sustained the interest of the London public by writing three
articles of his own about the visit for the *Advertiser*.[2]

Bucke's own reactions to the visit are especially significant. His letters to Harry Buxton Forman make it clear
that he found himself in the perplexing but exhilarating
situation of living on a day-to-day basis with a 'god-man'.
He took advantage of this intimacy to gather information
for his forthcoming biography. For example, during an ex-
cursion with Whitman along the St. Lawrence River, he
asked him why he had never married. Whitman's response
and Bucke's reaction to it are recorded in a letter from
Bucke to his wife. It seems that Whitman's visit to Canada
was both productive and enjoyable, and Bucke hoped that
it might become an annual event, but Whitman never did
return, apparently because of opposition from Bucke's wife
(letter 15).

Bucke had begun work on Whitman's biography before
this visit and continued to work on it (letters 8–24). At the
outset Bucke's notion of his biography was quite clear: it

would be the account of a man whose life and work exemplified and substantiated the thesis of *Man's Moral Nature*. In a circular he solicited information from Whitman's friends and acquaintances. Publication of the facts of the poet's life, together with a correct reading of his poems, would establish Whitman, Bucke believed, as the supreme example of the evolution of the moral nature. It may be seen that in his plans Bucke was more inclined to hagiography than biography.

Bucke's scheme might well have been carried out if Whitman had not been alive, or even if he had been the sort to sit back and allow others to shape his image; but perhaps most characteristic of Whitman's verse and prose is the celebration of the self, and although the self thus celebrated underwent several transformations, Whitman seems to have had no desire to serve as an exemplar of the evolution of man's moral nature. Bucke was, in fact, worried that Whitman, who heavily revised and rewrote the work, might obliterate all traces of his thesis. Then too, Whitman's ideas of biography were radically different from Bucke's. In 1882, upon receiving a copy of Franklin B. Sanborn's *Henry David Thoreau,* Whitman wrote Sanborn: 'The telling of Life after all refuses to be put in a polish'd, formal, consecutive statement—better, living glints, samples, autographic letters above all, memoranda of friends &c— You have pursued this plan & the result justifies—Froude's late *"Carlyle"*, a precious book, pursues it too—& succeeds—' (WW 1175). To William D. O'Connor he suggested that he collect all his writings on him: 'there is something to me quite preferable in these *collectanea* at first hand for a life, affair, even history, out of which the modern intelligent reader, (a new race unknown before our time) can take and adapt & shape for him or herself—' (WW 1183).

Bucke's *Walt Whitman* may perhaps be most accurately described, to use Whitman's term, as collectanea, the first part of the book dealing with Whitman's life and the second with his works. In the first chapter Bucke does little more than present a setting for the reminiscences of others, including the poet himself. Bucke points out that the best source for Whitman biography is Whitman: 'What he was, how he lived, kept himself up during these years, and how at the end partially recuperated, is so well set forth by himself in *Specimen Days,* that it would be mere impertinence for any one else to attempt to retell the tale' (p. 47). The second and third chapters are largely based on Whitman's visit with Bucke in 1880. They give a minute physical description of Whitman and make some attempt at an interpretation of his personality. Bucke approvingly reports the theory of an unnamed friend of Whitman's: 'there are two natures in Walt Whitman. The one is of immense suavity, self-control, a mysticism like the occasional fits of Socrates, and a pervading Christ-like benevolence, tenderness, and sympathy. . . . But these qualities, though he has enthroned them, and for many years governed his life by them, are duplicated by far sterner ones. No doubt he has mastered the latter, but he has them' (p. 56). It is noteworthy that the 'far sterner' qualities are not discussed: indeed, Bucke asserts that the hostility of some toward Whitman is not caused by any flaw in the poet's work or life but rather by the perversity of his detractors. Those who heap abuse upon Whitman do so 'doubtless according to a morbid attribute in humanity, and one of its mysterious laws' (p. 58).

The picture of Whitman which emerges is both insipid and implausible. According to Bucke, Whitman's only vice is reading newspapers—all other temptations of both the flesh and spirit are conspicuous by their absence. This lack of vices is not balanced by vividly portrayed virtues. When Bucke selects incidents to illustrate Whitman's goodness, the result is cloying: 'He was especially fond of children. . . . Often the little ones, tired, and fretful, the moment he took them up and caressed them, would cease crying, and perhaps go to sleep in his arms' (p. 55).

Bucke's conception of Whitman's personality may be revealed in the frontispiece he selected for his book. Bucke felt that 'the sentiment of the intaglio frontispiece' was 'a pervading Christ-like benevolence' (p. 56). Edwin Haviland Miller, on the other hand, quite accurately describes this portrait as 'saccharine'.[3]

The bulk of Part I, however, focuses around William D. O'Connor's *The Good Gray Poet* (1865–66) and O'Connor's introductory letter, prepared especially for the biography. The pamphlet had been highly influential in creating the public image of Whitman, and Whitman had been pleased with O'Connor's work. While examining the proofs for the biography, he wrote to O'Connor: 'I have been looking through the G[ood] G[ray] P[oet] as Dr B sent it in his copy, & it comes to my soul over the dozen years more eloquent & beautiful than ever—seems to me, (as a passionate shooting shaft launched into those times, & indeed fitting to the whole situation then & since)—*it deserves to stand just as it is*—' (WW 1193). Bucke was wistful in his admiration for the pamphlet.

The second part of the biography is concerned with the history, reception, and interpretation of *Leaves of Grass*. For Bucke, this part—especially chapter III, in which he attempts to interpret the poems in the light of *Man's Moral Nature*—was the heart of the book. A history of the publication of the poems and a commentary on their meaning was to establish the canon and lay the basis for valid future interpretations of them.

Chapter 1, 'History of Leaves of Grass', is addressed both to a contemporary audience and to those to come, and this focus presents difficulties. Bucke wants to point out the great moral import of *Leaves of Grass*, but he also wants his contemporaries to buy the book. The result is unfortunate—at times he sounds more like an agent, or even a bookseller, than a disciple.[4] Here Bucke also points to, though he does not develop it, his thesis concerning the basic nature of *Leaves of Grass*. He believes that the work has a 'central secret', and that the 'key' to this secret is that it 'represents a man whose ordinary every-day relationship with Nature is such that to him mere existence is happiness' (p. 136). At this point Bucke has worked in, perhaps a little obliquely, one of central notions of *Man's Moral Nature*. It may be recalled that in the closing sentence of that book, he stated that whoever has a highly developed moral nature 'is more than wise—he is happy' (p. 200). Accordingly, the 'secret' of *Leaves of Grass* is that it expresses the life of the exalted moral nature. The bulk of the chapter, however, is concerned with a factual account of Whitman's publications from 1855 to 1882.

A mere summary of the second and third chapters will not do justice to what Bucke was attempting to do. Submerged, but present nonetheless, there is a direct application and development of the central ideas in *Man's Moral Nature*. Keeping in mind Bucke's original plans for this biography, we can read the second chapter as an extension of the ideas of the poet and poetry presented in *Man's Moral Nature*. For Bucke, the poet was someone supremely gifted with the positive faculty of love, and it was through his poems that he communicated this experience to others, who were elevated by it. However, from the beginning Bucke makes it clear that *Leaves of Grass* needs interpretation. Indeed, he goes so far as to select 'Shut Not Your Doors', a poem with a tolerably clear surface meaning, and declares that this poem 'could not be in any degree explained to a person who knew nothing of *Leaves of Grass*' (p. 158): '*Leaves of Grass* is made up of language which I have characterized as indirect, but which, when understood, is seen to be more direct than any other' (p. 163). To the contemporary reader, Bucke's method of explication is both unsettling and naive: he will quote a line or passage and then examine it for its 'meaning'. In all instances he moves from the specifics of Whitman's lines to the generalities of a philosophic system. His explication of one line from the opening of 'Song of Myself' and one from the closing should make clear his procedure:

> I have heard what the talkers were talking, the talk of the begin-
> ning and the end, means, I have studied what has been taught in
> the philosophies and religious systems as to the Creation or the
> final destinies and purposes of men and things. . . . and filter and
> fibre your blood means, and purify and strengthen your spiritual
> nature (pp. 161–63).

Yet Bucke's method is more complex than it may at first
appear. Accordingly, the interpretations Bucke presents in
Walt Whitman are not, as they may at first appear, simply
the products of the intellect; they are the distillations of
what has been experienced by the moral nature. The reader
of Whitman reacts primarily with his own moral nature,
and it is only upon reflection that he extracts intelligible
statements from his experience. To be appreciated, Bucke's
explications, which seem so conventional and thin, must
be viewed as resonating with an intense, but incommuni-
cable, emotional—that is, moral—richness. The reader of
'Song of Myself' 'is not merely told that . . . things are
good, and persuaded or argued into believing it (that has
been done a thousand times, and is a small matter), but he
is brought into contact with, and absolutely fused in the
mind of Walt Whitman . . . and as he reads the poem . . .
the state of mind of the author inevitably (in some measure) passes over to the reader, and he practically becomes
the author—becomes the person who thinks so, knows so,
feels so' (pp. 159–60).

Bucke also presents a further development of his theory
of the nature of the poet. In *Man's Moral Nature*, he defined
the poet as one who is supreme in the positive faculty of
love and the religious leader as one who is supreme in the
positive faculty of faith. In *Walt Whitman*, however, Bucke
makes faith the chief attribute of 'Song of Myself', which
he calls 'perhaps the most important poem that has so far
been written at any time, in any language' (p. 159): 'This
"Song of Myself" is, in the highest sense of the word, a
religious poem. From beginning to end it is an expression
of Faith, the most lofty and absolute that man has so far

attained. There are passages in it expressive of love or sympathy, but taken as a whole, the groundwork and vivifying spirit of the poem is Faith' (p. 163). In short, the central poem of *Leaves of Grass* is, for Bucke, sacred scripture, and its creator is a religious innovator.

After achieving this supreme position, Bucke believes, Whitman entered a decline. His analysis of this process also gives us a synopsis of his aesthetic theories. He thinks that the decline began with *Drum-Taps* (1865). He concedes that the poems are beautiful, but beauty is not to be the criterion of true poetry: 'They are, it is true, the most beautiful poems Walt Whitman has written . . . but they would never (not a thousand such poems) alter materially for the better a human life' (p. 170). Critics who prefer these poems are misguided. Had Whitman pursued this course, he would have ended up as one of the 'great poets', a term which Bucke uses ironically and in quotation marks: 'A few more steps of the same length in the same direction, towards beauty of execution with loss of strength—towards fulness of expression with loss of suggestion—towards greater polish and facility of pleasing with loss of power of arousing and vivifying—and Walt Whitman would be upon the plane of the "great poets" of the nineteenth century. But, thank God, he can never take those steps. He is safe from this fate' (ibid.).

In one of the most interesting passages in the biography, Bucke compares Whitman to Satan after the fall: 'In "Drum-Taps" Walt Whitman's genius has "not yet lost all its original brightness, nor appears less than Archangel ruined" ' (p. 170).[5] To Bucke, the poet of the first three editions of *Leaves of Grass* was a divine figure. For relinquishing his faith and taking on more human attributes, however, he was expelled from heaven. Though still towering above all others, he is no longer divine: 'The splendid faith of the earlier poems is not extinct . . . but it is greatly dimmed. On the other hand, love and sympathy are as strongly expressed here as anywhere else in *Leaves of Grass* . . . the tears shed

by Walt Whitman in writing these poems, while they indicate to us clearly the passionate sympathy which dictated
them, show also a loss of personal force (*i.e.* faith) in the
man who some years before wrote "Children of Adam" and
"Calamus" without flinching' (p. 171).

The biography concludes with an appendix of twenty-
four reviews of *Leaves of Grass*. Whitman had included
various reviews in the second edition, and in 1860 he
issued *Leaves of Grass Imprints*, a collection of reviews, including the famous Emerson letter, as an advertisement for
the book, so Bucke was following a practice Whitman himself established at the very start of his career.

Bucke's *Walt Whitman* is neither the thesis book the author set out to write nor a conventional biography. To a
large extent his text serves merely as the framework for a
wide collection of documents, and the book is really a
rather loosely organized sourcebook of biographical and
bibliographical data. Whitman was pleased with the result,
and five years later, when it appeared that he was dying,
he urged Bucke not to alter the biography in any way:

> Of late I have two or three times occupied spells of hours or two
> hours running over with best & alertest sense & mellowed & rip-
> ened by five years your 1883 book (biographical & critical) about
> me & L of G—& my very deliberate & serious mind to you is that
> you *let it stand just as it is*—& if you have any thing farther to write
> or print book shape, you do so in an *additional* or further annex (of
> say 100 pages to its present 236 ones)—leaving the present 1883
> vol. intact as it is, any verbal errors excepted—& the further pages
> as (mainly) reference to and furthermore &c. of *the original vol.*—
> the text, O'C[onnor]'s letters, the appendix—every page of the 236
> left as now—This my spinal and deliberate request— (WW 1799).

Bucke complied.

The years between 1883 and 1888 were uneventful. Whitman's health continued to decline, but so slowly that there
was no need for immediate concern. The biography was
reprinted in 1884 in Scotland with a section, edited by Edward Dowden, devoted to the English critics of Whitman;

but Bucke published nothing in these intervening years. His literary work may have been impeded by his own ill heath. On 4 January 1886, he wrote to Harry Buxton Forman: 'As regards my own health, I am of course poorly, feeling pretty miserable a good part of the time; have been in this state for over a year, in fact nearly or quite two years. But I got very bad last summer and autumn. Lately I am not suffering quite so much, don't seem to have any disease, just tired out, poor appetite, and low spirits.'[6] Most of the letters from Bucke to Whitman dating from these years appear to be lost, and those which do survive deal to a large extent with the commonplace details of everyday life.

(8)

To Walt Whitman

[London,] Jan 19th [18]80

My dear Walt

I am going to ask a great favor of you—I want you to write me a sketch of your interior life—especially in relation to the conception and elaboration of "Leaves of Grass" [—] The germanancy and groth of such a product as "Leaves of Grass" is a psycological expression almost unique in the history of the race and some record of it ought to remain if possible—I need not explain any further what I want from you for you will understand at once what I mean and you must surely have often thought of putting it upon record[1]

I hope you will take this matter into serious and favourable consideration[2]

And I am

Faithfully yours
R M Bucke

[1]This letter provides an approximate date for the beginning of Bucke's biography.
[2]Apparently Whitman responded only by sending Bucke a list of materials to use in writing the biography (letter of 3 February).

(9)

To Walt Whitman

[London,] Feb 3ᵈ [18]80

My dear Walt

I have Burrough's book and also his last article in "Birds & Poets".[1] I have O'Connor's "Good Gray Poet" parts of which are beautifull—I have Mrs. Gilchrists letter in the "Radical."[2] All these and *anything* else I can get on this subject are interesting, and will be more or less usefull, to me—but what I *specially* want just now is new facts about the *man*—both bearing upon his inward and outward life— I hope you will give me any help in reason that you can in this direction.

I hope that your brothers will do something for me and I hope that if you have any thing to say about it you will encourage them to do something[3]—I will return the little pamphlet[4] after awhile meantime I will take good care of it & be sure not to lose it

Yours always

R M Bucke[5]

---

[1]John Burroughs, *Notes on Walt Whitman as Poet and Person* (1867); 'The Flight of the Eagle' (1877).

[2]William Douglas O'Connor, *The Good Gray Poet, A Vindication* (1866); Anne Gilchrist, 'An Englishwoman's Estimate of Walt Whitman' (1870). In the biography Bucke reprinted *The Good Gray Poet* and extracts from 'An Englishwoman's Estimate'.

[3]Although Whitman at this time was living with George Washington Whitman at 431 Stevens Street, there was not much sympathy between the brothers. Some notion of the attitude of the family may be gained from the interview with George Washington Whitman that Traubel conducted in 1893 ('Notes from Conversations with George W. Whitman, 1893: Mostly in his Own Words', *In Re*, pp. 33–40). Discussing the publication of the first edition of *Leaves of Grass*, George remarked: 'I was about twenty-five then. I saw the book—didn't read it all—didn't think it worth reading—fingered it a little. Mother thought as I did— did not know what to make of it' (p. 35).

[4]Possibly *The Good Gray Poet*.

[5]The Whitman letter to which Bucke is responding is apparently lost. Miller lists a missing letter from Whitman to Bucke of 26 Janaury 1880 (*Corr.*, III, 434).

(10)

To Jessie Bucke

Washington
May 31st 1880
Monday morning

My darling Jessie

I have been here since friday evening staying with Mr
Gorsh—I think I shall remain here two days yet that is
untill some time on Wednesday—I shall return then to
Phil^a and on thursday evening (as I told you in my last
which I hope you received) Walt and I will start for Canada
when I hope to find your dear self and all the sweet little
ones well and merry. You will of course have the best spare
room made ready for Walt, I wish we could give him still
better accommodation, no palace that ever was built would
be quite good enough for Walt, but we must at least give
him the best we have and along with that give him our
love and he will be satisfied for indeed he is easy enough
to please if he feels he is liked, I suppose Bessie is with you
now if so give her my love [/] tell her she has lost her
chance of catching Walt by getting engaged in the reckless
hasty way she did.

I shall be home I think without fail on friday evening—if
I am not I shall write again or telegraph—I have had no
letters from you my darling since I left except the two I
mentioned the last time I wrote but I hope to find several
waiting for me when I return to Phil^a [—] I hope Miss Mary
is taking her cod liver oil and that she is getting better [/] if
she does not soon get stronger she will have to stop giving
lessons to the "Good little Soul" and that I suppose would
break her poor little heart—give her my love, Kiss the children for me

I am
My dearest Jessie

Your most affectionate
husband
R M Bucke

(11)

To Harry Buxton Forman

London, June 6th 1880

My dear Harry:

Have your letter of April 30, and May 1st and wish to say that I take all mine back and am so sorry now that I wrote it—I mean mine of April 14th, but the fact is that I thought you must be disgusted with the "Agency" as you call it and wanted to get rid of it; Of course I forget now exactly what I did say but I know that I was really annoyed that I could not get answers to my letters and no books. Some of the books I asked you for I wanted to buy on a recent trip to the States and I did not like to for fear that I might find duplicates here from you on my return. This has happened in a few instances when I have asked you for a book and after several months I have given up the notion of your sending it— bought it here, then received it from you. No odds about all this I should not have allowed myself to become annoyed at you for you have been in a great deal of trouble for me first and last without having much return for it—and I should not have been annoyed about the business part of the matter, but I kept fancying that you found the business part of the orders a nuisance and wished me and them at Old Harry. But we won't say anything more about it. I have more important things to talk about. I returned the day before yesterday from New York, Phila, and Washington and Walt came home with me—he will spend a large part of the summer here and we will probably go to Montreal, Ottawa, etc. together before the summer is over. I have not yet made up my mind whether Walt is human or divine—this makes associating with him a little embarrasing at times, however he is so entirely lovable that one is inclined not to care too much whether he is God or not—If one was sure he was a man one could not love him any better—and if one was sure he was a god, one could not respect and esteem him more highly—so you see the matter is simpler than it seems at first sight. While I was away I worked like a beaver collecting materials, and putting myself in a position to collect materials for my work on Walt. (1) I found and procured all Walt's early writings, mostly of '41, '42, and '45—they are essays and stories and do not seem to be of much literary value. (2) I procured and got on the track of [?]—so I shall procure, a great many newspapers and magazine articles on Walt and on "Leaves of Grass" so that I think I shall soon have everything which is reasonably connectable and of any importance in this line—I find that a great deal has been written of Walt in Danish, Norwegian, Swedish and Hungarian magazines; this material is largely out of my reach but I shall procure some of it and have it translated. (3) I have called upon and become pretty well acquainted with a number of friends of Walt's and have got promises from quite a number of them of assistance. In the way of answers to my circular (which I enclose) and in other ways, in particular, I found a man in Washington,[1]—he is a baggageman on the Baltimore & Potomac R. R. who has been an intimate friend of Walt's for 15 years—he and Walt love one another (as far as I can make out) much more than father and son can love one another—this man has had letters from Walt for 15 years, and of course saved them all,—he had a trunk full of them, these letters I hope to get—he will send them to me and I shall keep them as long as I like—I hope to make a long chapter of extracts from them. (4) Besides all of this I shall have this summer a chance to study the man himself. If I cannot write a book worth reading then I am as I have sometimes suspected a blasted idiot and that's the end of it.

I enclose you Trubner's account,[2] please attend to this little matter. The business connected with the sale of "Man's Moral Nature" is not so large as to be very oppresive even to a man so busy as yourself. That was a nice notice in MIND which you sent me. Walt says I must print it as an advertisement in the N. Y. Tribune, and I suppose I shall. Now about books—I have received "The Light of Asia";[3] "Song of Songs" and Barnes Poems and in fact all the books in your account. We had better now make a new start and as I order a book I will put it down, so do not send anything I do not ask for in this or future letters. You

will send me of course your Shelley's PROSE as soon as it
is out and if possible in a shape to match POETRY. Anything in the current magazines you can pick up about Walt
will be always welcome and may be considered a standing
order. You must not go to any trouble about old Mag.
articles, I think I am on the road to get all of them. However, [any] you come across, buy, and send me on the
chance that I have not seen it.—I have got the "Sacred Book
of the East".[4] I have "Imprints of Leaves of Grass" but do
not own it. I am advertising for it. If you can get hold of a
copy send it to me. I shall send you photos of the children
as soon as we have them done. We have been out for a
long time but must get some more soon. We do not get
Macmillans but I shall buy the April No. to get your article.
Your Shelley will be a great work. It will keep your name
fresh for hundreds of years, for there is no question yours
will be the Shelley. It is a great thing to have accomplished
such a work as that. I shall certainly come to England in a
very few years if I live (perhaps next year.) Of course I
cannot go this year as Walt is here and I hope will be here
all summer. When I do come we will have a big time. You
will have to quit work and we will go for a run on the
Continent. Old Duke Street will not be a circumstance to it.
I am twice as young as I used to be in those time[s]—Lord,
I fancy I used to be quite an old man then. I send you some
MS of Walt's to put you in good humor. Stir your stump
now and attend to my orders or I will send you a devilish
sight worse letter next time. Walt sends you his kind regards. He says you must not think any the less of him
because he does not write—writing is very difficult to him
and he has a good deal that he is forced to do—he writes
VERY little to anyone. My love to you—goodby

R. M. Bucke

[1]Peter Doyle.
[2]Trübner & Co. were the British agents for *Man's Moral Nature*.
[3]Sir Edwin Arnold, *The Light of Asia, or The Great Renunciation* (London, 1879).
[4]*The Sacred Books of the East*, ed. F. Max Muller, 50 vols. (Oxford, 1879–1910).

(12)

To Jessie Bucke

Asylum for the Insane
Kingston
Aug. 2. 1880

My darling Jessie

Walt and I stayed at the Hub House again last night, and this morning we returned to the Asylum in the steamer "Princess Louise" [/] I have sent you a paper which gives a map of the Park and I have marked on it the position of the Hub House—which stands on a little mote of an island a few hundred yards from the "Park"—the paper will give you an idea of what they do at the "Park".— I fully expected to get a letter from you my dear girl when I got home this morning but I was disappointed—however no doubt I shall get one this afternoon and that will be just as good—

Walt and I have enjoyed our stay here very much—last night on the verandah of the Hub House Walt and I had a long talk—I asked him how it was that he never got married—and whether he had remained single from a set purpose—He said "No, I have done nothing of set purpose"— he said he supposed the chief reason he never married was that he had an instinct against forming ties that would bind him to any thing—an instinct to freedom and absolute unconstraint—He seemed to think that he had done right not to marry, but that he had nevertheless been personally a great loser by not having had a wife and children.[1] But I do not think he regards his own happiness much,—he regards what he thinks is right a thousand times more—but it is the old story—"Seek ye first the Kingdom of God and his righteousness, and *all things else shall be added unto you.*"—Walt is happy and the principal reason he is happy is because he does not seek for happiness itself but for something higher the attainment of which *involves* the attainment of happiness—Goodly my sweet one—If Sarah is with you give her my love—Kiss the

dear children for me—I send you a hundred kisses for yourself and I am

Always your loving husband

R M Bucke

[1]Bucke has recorded this conversation in the biography, where he adds the following comment: 'Yes, it was the instinct of self-preservation. Had you married
at the usual age, *Leaves of Grass* would never have been written' (p. 60).

(13)

To Harry Buxton Forman

London, Sept. 17 1880

My dear Harry:

I have your letter of August 7th and also your postcard
of 17th. Also Shelley's prose, also the copies of "Leaves of
Grass Imprints" for which I am much obliged to you
though I had a couple of copies sent to me by Mr. Child
of Trubner & Co. I have looked into the prose a little, all I
could—so far, and am very much pleased with what I
have seen. I am very glad to have it and glad that it is
out, so that you may have it off your hands and be able to
take a rest which I hope you will do for a time. I suppose
I ought to send you some money as I must be considerably behind with you, but I will not send any until my
next letter reached you. Walt is still with me. He leaves on
the 28th instant, I shall go with him as far as "The Falls"
and see him off from there. I can say nothing to you
about him except that the three-and-a-half months' absolute intimacy in which we have just lived have made him
seem greater to me than he did before, which I hardly
thought possible. I have made a great many notes during
his residence here of conversations, habits, manners, etc.
etc. which I will go to work on after he is gone, and make
into a book along with my lecture on W. W. and other
material. I ought by rights be able to produce an exact

picture of the man to leave for coming generations as well as for use of that which is current now. I have a lot of material which I will hardly be able to use at present but which I hope to use in subsequent Eds;—Should I live after Walt leaves us. I have especially a series of letters written by Walt to a young man, one of his most intimate friends of Walt's, and doubtless, as times go, by [and by] I shall get many other things of great interest. The letters I speak of are wonderful, they are extremely simple, but have an extraordinary charm which I could not give you any idea of. You are right not to send me Todhunter on Shelley[1] or any other book unless I order it—this book I have ordered and I would have had two copies of it if you had sent it. I should like you to send me "Ward's English Poets" the two Vols. now out and the others when they appear—also the "Secular Review" for March 20, 1880. It has an article on W. W. that I should very much like to see.[2] (N. B.) It is published, 84 Fleet Street. Is not the last vol. of Renan's "Origines du Christianisme" out yet? That is Vol. 2, of "Les Evangiles?"[3] If it is, please send it. I should like to have Renan's "Hibbert (?) Lectures"[4] in French of course.

I wish I could be with you in Paris. I think I should enjoy it intensely seeing life in the streets, the theatres, the picture galleries. I should go and see Victor Hugo if I could get an entre or whatever you call it. I have been reading his "Legende des Sciecles"[5] a good deal this summer and have got up a good deal of interest in him. There is one other book I want you to send me as soon as convenient, and that is Keat's Letters to Fanny Browne.[6] I have a copy as you know which you gave me but I need another for a special purpose. I cant say that I take a special interest in your Keats though I will of course have to have a copy when it comes out—not however, a fearfully expensive one like the Shelley. I don't suppose I ever saw the real value of Keats for some reason. I have read him a good deal too. I once read "Endymion" through. I thought, and think still, that it was a most wonderful achievement. Goodby.

I send you my love.

R. M. Bucke

[1]John Todhunter, *A Study of Shelley* (London, 1880).
[2]W. Hale White, 'The Genius of Walt Whitman', *Secular Review*, 20 March 1880.
[3]Joseph Ernest Renan, *Histoire des origines du Christianisme*, vol. 5: *Les Évangiles et la seconde génération chrétienne* (Paris, 1877).
[4]*Conférences d'Angleterre, Rome et le Christianisme* (Paris, 1880).
[5]Victor Marie Hugo, *La Légende des siècles*, 5 vols. (Paris, 1859–83).
[6]*Letters of John Keats to Fanny Brawne, Written in the Years 1819 and 1820, and Now Given from the Original Manuscripts, with Introduction and Notes by H. B. Forman* (London, 1878).

(14)

To Harry Buxton Forman

London, May 22d, 1881

My dear Harry:

My book "WALT WHITMAN, a STUDY" is done and copies out ready for the printer, but Walt will have to see it before I send it off. I am almost expecting to see him here any day but he may not come after all, if he does not, something must be devised. I will send the MSS as soon as I can. Want to have the book out in good time this Fall. How does the picture for the book get on?[1] Please let me know at once and be sure I get a copy as soon as possible for I am very anxious to see it. We may want to see the picture by the end of July or middle of August. I can count on the delivery of them in N. Y. by that time? I will instruct you where to send them in N. Y. before you ship them for though I expect Putnam's Sons will be my publisher I am not certain of it. We are going to have a University (the Western University) in London (this London) right off. It is to be opened in October and I am just at it nów. I think I shall succeed and I will probably take a chair myself. If I do, I shall probably take "Nervous and Mental

Diseases" but I will tell you more about this later. No chance of seeing England THIS year but I am determined to see you all before a very great while.

I am always

Affectionately yours,
R. M. Bucke

P. S. I have never seen that "well written" German Novel.

---

[1]Forman had suggested the frontispiece for the book in a letter of 4 March 1881:

> There is a life-sized chalk drawing over here by young [Herbert H.] Gil-christ which I prefer as a work of art, and even as a portrait, it is quite the opposite of that one of yours in every way. It represents Walt just come in from walking, seated with his two hands grasping his stick; his chin is on his chest and his eyes almost, if not quite closed, but the benevolence and grandeur of the face and the flowing beauty of the white hair and beard, are most striking. Walt calls it—"The Homeric Tramp" (Seaborn).

(15)

To Jessie Bucke

Asylum for the Insane
London
June 19, 1881

My dearest Jessie

I have written to Walt Whitman and have done my best to stop him from coming here without being absolutely rude to him. I wish you had said long ago that you did not want him, but I was under the impression that you liked him—you seemed to, and I knew you had good reason to. Some of our Sarnia friends have been cautioning you against him and you have been weak enough to fall into their way of thinking. You may be sure I shall never try to get Walt Whitman into any house where he is not wanted, and I am more sorry than I can say that he is likely to come here this summer—If he comes now I shall have no plea-sure in his visit—at first I thought I would enclose your letter to him but that seemed too hard on you and cruel to him so I have taken a different course and one that I hope will prevent his coming without letting him see that we don't want him for I want him as little as you do now—But Jessie never allow yourself to imagine for a moment that you or any of you can shake my affection for Walt Whitman—If all the world stood on one side, and Walt Whitman and general contempt on the other and I had to choose which I would take I do not think I should hesitate (I hope I should not) to choose Walt Whitman.

Do not be uneasy, you could not make me angry on such a subject but I am profoundly grieved to see that our minds are so far apart upon it—

The girls send their love to you and Mr Beddoe wishes to be kindly remembered

I am your affectionate

husband
R M Bucke

(16)

To William Douglas O'Connor

Asylum for the Insane
London—Ont
June 27. 1881

My dear O'Connor

If I had written you a dozen letters without an answer yours of 21st inst. would have well paid for them all. I am glad you like the etching [/] upon receipt of your letter I decided to use it—I myself liked [it] very much from the first but I did not propose to act entirely on my own judgement in such a matter for I know very little about pictorial art in any of its forms—I showed the picture to a great many people here who knew Walt when he was with me last summer, some liked it but most condemned it, as a rule however they were not judges—I then sent a copy to Burroughs, one to Johnston, and one to you and made up my mind I would be guided by what you said. I purposely did not say to any of you what I thought about it—Johnston condemned the picture root and branch—Burroughs said a good deal for it and a good deal against it, the *pro* outweighing the *con*— then you approved it and that settled the matter. Since hearing from you I have a line from Walt to say that he likes it which is satisfactory so that matter is settled—To meet the views however of those who do not care for the etching and who think a *Photo* would be better I am going to use a photo *also*—the etching will go in the front of the book and the photo which was taken here last summer will go in the chapter called "Walt Whitman in 1880" [/] As for Stedman and his article[1] we can afford to forget them both now and especially since contemtible as the latter was I fancy it did far more good than harm—of course you saw the N. Y. Star's review of Stedman? If I recollect right it consisted of ten words as follows: "Stedman on Walt Whitman—A man milliner writing about Sampson." We will let it go at that remembering what Goethe said in a similar case: Hat doch der Wallfisch seine Laus Muss auch die meine haben. [—] If you only carry out your intentions in re "The Good Gray Poet" you will make me a happy man—I am very glad that you are going over it again although I was well content with it as it was—still I have no doubt you will make improvements— you rate the work altogether too low—certainly it was written for an occation, but that occation, and (if I am not mistaken) the "Good Gray Poet" which it calls forth will live in the minds of men for many a long year—People who *know* Walt Whitman rate your pamphlet very highly—this might be the case if the pamphlet itself had no extraordinary merit, merely an account of its subject—but I find (what is more to the purpose as regards the literary excellence of your work) that people who do not know Walt Whitman at all see its greatness and feel its power—if all of my book could have the merits of this part of the appendix to it I should feel confident for its future.

The last two pages of your letter—in re Miss Platt—gave me as good a laugh as I have had many a day—My dear fellow I w^d like well enough to send you the lady's letters but in the first place you would find them very stupid and in the second place I cannot honorably do it—you may safely trust this matter in my hands—When I issued my circular I cast my net in the waters to catch fish of all kinds as many as I could—but *I never agreed to eat them all*—of course I got some sheepheads and dogfish in my haul but I got also (as you will see by and by) some perfect beauties at the same time—Goodly my dear fellow—whatever you do don't forget or neglect the "Good Gray Poet" and the *preface to it*—the great object of which, remember, is to show clearly your present attitude towards Leaves of Grass and Walt Whitman

I am your friend

R M Bucke

[1]Edmund Clarence Stedman published an article on Whitman in *Scribner's Magazine* for November 1880.

(17)

To Walt Whitman

[London] 9ᵗʰ May [18]82

Copy

Dear Walt

I have the file of Osgood correspondence from O'Connor—so this is American freedom at the end of the 19ᵗʰ Century, is it?[1] I do not know what to say or do, the more I think about it the worse I feel. The papers here would hardly take the matter up in any shape, nor would it (it seems to me) do much good if they did. [—] No American paper (judging from past experience) would print any thing I might write on the subject. The only thing I can think of to do is to have the correspondence just forwarded me by O'Connor printed with some comments of my own and send it broadcast to your friends here and in England and to the press. Would you object to this being done? or would Osgood have any right to object to his letter being printed? I have to be away from home from May 22ᵈ to June 6ᵗʰ (about), but it would not be too late to attend to it when I got back and it would give O'Connor time to fire his first shot before the matter was made any more public than it is now.

To do as I propose might have the effect of making it slightly warm for the Philistines, no doubt some of the papers would take it up and it would not do the sale of the book any harm whoever published it.

Please let me know at once what you think of my plan Your friend

R M Bucke

---

[1]On 1 March 1882, Oliver Stevens, the district attorney of Boston, notified Osgood and Co., the publishers of the seventh edition (1881–82) of *Leaves of Grass*, that Whitman's book was officially classified as obscene and was to be suppressed. O'Connor's letter of support for Whitman, referred to here, appeared in the New York *Tribune* on 25 May 1882, and Bucke's letter to the editor of the Springfield, Mass., *Republican* was printed on 23 May 1882. Bucke's letter and extracts from O'Connor's are reprinted in his biography of Whitman (pp. 229–30 and 150–52).

(18)

To William Douglas O'Connor

[Cincinnati,] 30th May [188]2

My dear O'Connor

I have been in Ottawa for a week attending a meeting of the new "Royal Society of Canada[.]" I got home yesterday at noon for *an hour and a half* then left for here. I got your letter and a copy of the "Tribune" sent me by McWaters. Your letter is grand, it hits hard and in the right spot, it will undoubtedly do an immense amount of good both to W. W. and to the general cause of free letters, I cannot express to you with what entheusiasm I read and reread it—I send you today a copy of the Springfield Republican containing a very much weaker attempt of my own in the same direction in which your giant blows are struck—Now about my book upon which subject you naturally feel a little impatient [/] the explanation of the delay is as follows (and you will see that the explanation involves an embarrasment that may become serious): I was not in a position to negociate for its publication untill I could send the copy complete to a publisher hence I hurried you—when I got the whole copy together I sent it to my former publisher Putnams Sons [/] they did not care for it. I then (long before I heard a word about the row) sent it to Osgood thinking that the publisher of L. of G. was the right man (I had only sent it to Putnam on account of his personal request to me to do so and never thought that he would care to publish)—after sending it to Osgood I waited nearly two months (heard not a word) then wrote, they answered that James R. Osgood was in Europe and they were not prepared to say any thing untill his return which was expected about June 1st and asked to be allowed to retain the M.S. I told them to retain it but to let me know as soon as possible after the 1st June what they proposed in the case. [—] Now the devil of it is that this last row *must* go in the chapter on "The History of L. of G." and how can it be written in such a way that Osgood & Co will care to publish it? I *feel strong* that the book ought to be out—but how to get it out? If Osgood wants to publish how would it do to leave this last scrape out altogether for the present? If I insist upon putting it in and putting it in properly I must expect to look for another publisher and then more delay—I will keep you posted never fear but if you can advise me in the present juncture do so please[1]

Yours affectionately

R M Bucke

[1]With David McKay of Philadelphia as the publisher, Bucke was free to discuss the suppression. A section of chapter 1 of part 2 is subtitled 'The Attempted Official Suppression'.

(19: fragment)

To Walt Whitman

[12 June 1882 ?[1]]

The motto that you send for the title-page[2] would do

extremely well—meantime I had picked out one from *Lucretius* as follows:

> Quae cum magna multis miranda videtur
> gentibus humanis regio visendaque fertur,
> rebus optima bovis, multa munita virum vi,
> nil tamen hoc habuisse virs praeclarius in se
> nec sanctum magis et mirum carumque videtur
> carmina quin etiam divini pectoris eius
> vociferantur et exponunt praeclara reperta
> ut vix humana videatur stirpe creatus.

which being interpreted is:

Now though this great country is seen to deserve in many ways the wonder of mankind and is held to be well worth visiting, rich in all good things, guarded by large force of men, yet seems it to have held within it nothing more glorious than this man, nothing more holy marvellous and dear. The verses too of his godlike genuis cry with a loud voice and set forth in such wise his glorious discoveries that he hardly seems born of á mortal stock.

It is vulgarly supposed that by "this great country" Lucretius meant *Sicily* and by "this man" *Empedocles*; but it is plain enough that he really meant America and Walt Whitman—Any one can see that "Vociferantur" must have been intended to apply to the "barbaric Yawp". Isn't it so?

RMB.

Should I take the motto from Lucretius I am uncertain whether to use the latin or the translation—the latin of course w^d be the best but unfortunately so few read it.

---

[1]Although only the last two pages of this letter have survived, it may be dated with some certainty. On 10 June 1882, Whitman made the following entry in his 'Commonplace-Book': 'Sent letter to Dr Bucke, ab't "motif" of his book & ab't printing in Phila' (p. 225).

[2]Whitman's 'motto' is not known. He rejected this quotation from Lucretius (*De Rerum Natura* 1.726–33), and Bucke acquiesced (see letter 23). Bucke was fond of the quotation, however, and after Whitman's death he used his translation of it for the title page of *In Re* (1893).

(20)

To Harry Buxton Forman

London, 19th February
1883

My dear Harry:

The agreement to publish my book on W. W. is signed and I suppose we shall go to press at once and come out in six or eight weeks.

Will you kindly order the 1,000 copies of the Photo-Intaglio AND THE PLATE to be carefully packed and sent AT ONCE (by mail if possible, otherwise as you may direct) to David McKay, No. 23 South 9th Street, Philadelphia, Penn. U. S. A.

R. M. Bucke

(21)

To Walt Whitman

[London], 18th March [188]3

My dear Walt

I return you today the proof in *pages* [/] I have considered it all very carefully and am quite satisfied as to the re-arrangement of pages, pictures &c. please leave them as I have put them—I have not made much change—the burial scenes *must* face different pages as they will only be known as described in "List of Illustrations" by that fact—It would not do to print on back of photo-intaglio so I have added a leaf—the photo-intaglio will face /title/ page—the birth-house /will face/ opening of chap I (p. 13)—the "remote" and "immediate" "ancestry" pages I have moved as you will see—Van Velsor burial /hill/ picture will face p. 15, and W. burial hill picture p. 17—Portrait of father will face p. 26 (mention of his death)—every thing else is left as you put it. [—] I want portrait of Mother to face mention of her death (towards end of chap I)—then the photograph or phototype of W. W. /in 1880/ of writing should face page in that chap. where handwriting is mentioned. You told me

McKay could get the pictures printed in Phila at $1.80 or
$2 p.m.[1] have a letter from M^{c}K. in which he says Sher-
man & Co would charge me $20. p.m. for *three*, however,
no matter, they are ordered at De Vinnes N. Y. and will
be done immediately. I like all your emendations, additions, &c so far (on the whole) very much, I can see that
you are materially improving the book, for wh I feel very
gratefull—But dear Walt be very carefull like a good fellow with chap iii of part ii[2]—whatever you do dont slash
it up [/] if you make material changes send me the M. S.
with proofs that I may see exactly what they are and consider them—don't fail me in this—that chap is the pivot
on which the Book turns

R M Bucke

[1]An abbreviation for 'proof positive'.
[2]Here Bucke presented a religious interpretation of *Leaves of Grass*. Despite his
plea, facsimiles of the Maggin MS show that Whitman heavily revised this section
(see Quentin Anderson, ed., *Whitman's Autograph Revisions*, pp. 101, 102, 107,
111, 113, 115, 116, 119, 121, 123, and 125).

(22)

To Walt Whitman

[London,] 20th March [188]3

My dear Walt

I have this afternoon received, read, and remailed to you
galleys 37 to 45 inclusive. I open and read these parcels of
proof in fear and trembling (you must go as easy as you
can, you are the terrible surgeon with the knife & saw and
I am the patient). You left out my remarks on "children of
Adam",[1] I believe they were good but I acquiesce—your
additions are excellent as they have been all through. I
shall not feel half comfortable untill I have had the proof of
the rest of p[t] ii and have seen how much of me will be
left. Poor O'Connor too, he had to submit to the fatal
shears[2]—but you are going to make a book of it (if that is

possible) so go ahead if we do flinch. But still, for the Lord's sake, spare my ch iii pt ii as much as possible. I want you please (if I am not speaking to late) to save the M. S. and send it all to me when you are done with it. I shall be glad to have plate proofs as fast as made, if I see any thing in them that needs correcting will notify you other- wise will just put them by—I suppose you do not want them returned? It is still *winter* here, lots of snow, good sleighing,

R M Bucke

[1]For Whitman's deletions see Harold Jaffe, 'Richard Maurice Bucke's *Walt Whit- man;* Edited, with an Introduction and Variant Readings' (Ph.D. diss., New York University, 1968), pp. 196–200.
[2]Whitman altered O'Connor's paragraphing.

(23)

To Walt Whitman

[London,] 28th May [188]3

My dear Walt

I have had the book a couple of days and have looked through it, I believe it will do, and if it will the Editor will deserve more credit than the Author—I am really surprised at the tact and judgement you have displayed in putting my rough M. S. into shape and I am more than satisfied with all you have done—I see now that you were right about the Latin motto (as about every thing else)—it is *not* in line with the book and is better out of it. I should like to know who will be the English Pub^r and when the book will be published in England and when here? I suppose McKay will send me a statement (all in good time) showing my financial position as toward the vol.?

We are well here, the season is backward, the leaves not fully out yet; indeed the oaks and even some of the maples and elms have scarcely begun to come out yet—however the asylum grounds look lovely, we have had a great deal

of rain and the grass and the young leaves are exquisitely
fresh and green
Affectionately Yours

R M Bucke

(24)

To Walt Whitman

[London,] 9th Sept [188]3

Dear Walt

I have your card of Aug. 30. Yes, all right—I am satisfied
with "Walt Whitman" except that it does not express one
tenth what it ought to do justice to the subject, but I be-
leive it is the best I can do after all and so it must go—as
for the paying part of the business I am quite easy abt.
that—I think it will pay in the long run and if it does not I
am equally satisfied except that I would like it to have some
circulation on the chance of doing some good. [—] Yes, I
saw the Santa Fé letter too (thanks for it), and I also saw the
N. Y. Times of Aug 8th on it—did you see it?[1] was it not
shamefull? The man glories in his want of sympathy, and
laughs consumedly that any one else should have any. I saw
Tommy Nicholson down town yesterday and he showed me
your letter to him.[2] I was well pleased to see that you really
have some notion of paying us another visit—I hope to see
you next month and then perhaps we can arrange something—perhaps you will return with me, who knows, there
may be luck in store for me yet! and you think "breaking up
where you are living"? But you must tell me all about it
when I see you, please goodness that will be soon—but I
cannot tell yet when I can get away East, there are many
things to do first and a great deal to think of—will let you
know all about it when I know myself—
Goodly dear Walt

Your friend
R M Bucke

[1]On 20 July Whitman sent the citizens of Santa Fe, New Mexico, a letter of congratulation on the 'anniversary of the 333d year of the settlement of their city by the Spanish' (*Prose Works*, II, 552). On 8 August the New York *Times* quoted excerpts from the piece, concluding with the following comment:

> Thus his wide arms extending, WALT scoops in the Spaniard and the Indian and their product, composite of both the half-breed. The Greaser he hails, the horse-thief, the three-card monte man he hails, the dead beat, the mixed promiscuous loafer, sunning himself alongside of an adobe wall, inhaling cigarritos, he calls him camerado. The squaw, also, mate, of the Greaser, her he scoops in, her sees incorporate in America, her moving on half drunk to greater destinies than of Greece or feudal Europe. The Mexican priest he sees join in the procession of these States, falling in behind the Italian rag-picker, alongside the Chinaman, tucking up his skirts sacerdotal to keep ahead of the Polish Jew. Oh Mannahatta!

[2]Tomas Nicholson was an employee of the London Asylum whom Whitman met on his visit to Canada.

4

'*Millions of eyes in the future will watch our actions today*'

In the spring of 1888 two events occurred which radically changed the relationship between disciple and master. On 28 March Horace Traubel permanently altered the scope and nature of Whitman biography. For some time he had been taking notes of his visits with Whitman, but at the suggestion of his fiancée he began to expand these notes into a coherent narrative. He accumulated a vast collection of documents, mostly letters to Whitman—both the ones Whitman had saved and the ones he was then receiving almost daily. Whitman was, of course, aware of what Traubel was doing and quietly encouraged the project by granting him daily interviews and supplying him with documents. He also created an element of suspense by promising from time to time to reveal to Traubel the great secret of his life. Since Whitman and Traubel usually discussed the letters Whitman received, we are presented with what may be considered a transcript of a daily symposium. Through his letters, Bucke is one of the most frequent voices at these meetings.

Underlying all of Bucke's letters to Whitman of 1888–91 is the fact that the poet is dying. After the series of strokes Whitman suffered on 3 and 4 June 1888, there was no doubt about that fact. *Leaves of Grass* was in its final form by 1881, and Whitman was quite explicit about the nature of 'Sands at Seventy' and 'Good-Bye My Fancy'—they were 'annexes'. He devoted much of the latter part of 1888 to consolidating his position. In the winter of 1888, he issued what he called the 'big book', *Complete Poems & Prose of Walt Whitman, 1855–1888;* and earlier, in the letter to Bucke about his biography quoted above, he urged him not to tamper with its text.

Whitman's will of 28 June 1888, written at the instigation of Bucke, appointed Bucke, his lawyer friend Thomas Harned, and Traubel as literary executors. Bucke took his official responsibilities seriously. When it appeared that Herbert Gilchrist might be attempting to secure Whitman's literary executorship for himself or English associates, Bucke anxiously wrote to Traubel to be on the alert. During this period Bucke and Traubel also began to compile materials for *In Re Walt Whitman,* a work with many characteristics of a memorial volume. Bucke extended the rights given him in literary matters to the most personal details. He urged Traubel to secure the permission of Whitman's family to transfer the funeral arrangements for the poet from his relatives to his disciples, and even before a final location had been selected for Whitman's tomb, Bucke was busy with details for the services at the graveside.

Whitman's funeral is briefly described by Horace Traubel in 'At the Graveside of Walt Whitman'.[1] Except for the lack of music, the funeral ceremony was much as Bucke and Traubel planned it. There was no clergyman, and the chief speaker was Colonel Robert G. Ingersoll. Among the other speakers were Bucke and Harned. John Burroughs, who was present, did not speak. Bucke's funeral oration for Whitman was brief and stoical. In the concluding paragraph he said:

> In your own right you took rank here below as a supreme creative workman; in your own right to-day you take rank among the supreme creative gods.
>
> There in the highest regions of the ideal for countless ages your work will go on moulding into higher and yet more noble forms the spirit of man.
>
> Your life for me lit up the past with an auroral splendor, and upon the world's future you will shine a glorious sun, but the present is darkened by the somber shades of your setting.
>
> But our last word to you must not be a mournful one, whatever pain we may feel. Let it be rather a cry of exultation that you were given to the world, and that we have known you and know you.[2]

Bucke's real anguish at the death of his friend and master was expressed privately, in correspondence with the other disciples.

Much of the remainder of Bucke's life was devoted to the writing of *Cosmic Consciousness* and the editing of Whitman. A letter from him to Traubel indicates the nature and function of *In Re Walt Whitman*, published in 1893. In February 1892, when Whitman lay dying, Bucke wrote to Traubel that one of the functions of the work was to 'preëmpt the Walt Whitman market'. In the foreword Whitman's literary executors aptly style *In Re* as an 'Annex' to Bucke's *Walt Whitman*.

Bucke ran into difficulties, however, in his effort to publish his collections of Whitman's letters and literary fragments. Materials that were of intense interest to the disciples had, it would seem, little interest for the general literary public, and quite apart from the limited interest of commercial publishers in the letters of Whitman, there was the problem of their content. *Calamus*, containing the affectionate letters of a major poet to a streetcar conductor twenty-eight years his junior, might cause scandal. In a letter to Bucke Edward Carpenter points out the difficulties:

> Wallace [an English disciple] has forwarded on to me your proposed volume of Whitman letters to Peter Doyle. It has been to Kegan Paul & Co., & rejected. Nor do I think that there is the least chance of any London publisher taking it—both on account of the doubtfulness of the monetary speculation and the unheard of nature of the contents.
>
> But it is lovely—most excellent; and I am greatly in favor of publishing it. I have only been through it once, but I shall run over it again, & meanwhile I will give you some of my impressions. The interview with Peter is first-rate, full of suggestions & interest, & throwing light on a period of W's life so little known, it is priceless on that account alone; but anyhow it has the raciness & directness, so precious, of an *un*literary yet observant mind. The letters are most touching & feeling & full of interest; rather sad too after beg[innin]g. of '73—& help greatly to give one an idea of what Walt's heart was. . . . [3]

Plans for publishing in England did not materialize, and the next month Bucke wrote to Wallace: 'I want you to return the MS of "Calamus"—it seems likely that McKay will print it—if he will that is the best thing to do with it—better make him as far as possible the Walt Whitman publisher.'[4] McKay evidently refused, and the work was finally placed with Laurens Maynard of Boston. *Calamus* did, in fact, enjoy a modest sale and attracted a few prominent admirers, including John Addington Symonds and Henry James. In his review of the book, James pointed out: 'It has in a singular way something of the same relation to poetry that may be made out in the luckiest—few, but fine—of the writer's other pages; I call the way singular because it squeezes through the narrowest, humblest gate of prose.'[5]

Bucke had begun to plan an edition of *The Wound Dresser*[6] as early as 1893. On 11 March he wrote to Traubel: 'The

Hospital Letters cannot be "selected" on any terms—"*All or none*" is the word.'[7] Like *Calamus*, the book was published by Laurens Maynard, and Bucke was quite proud of it. He referred to the letters as 'immensely valuable'[8] and wrote that *The Wound Dresser* 'is one of the best books yet in which we see what kind of man Walt really was. I sincerely hope it will sell and be extensively read. Yes, we are getting Walt published at last and we deserve a lot of credit for it.'[9]

By publishing *Calamus* and *The Wound Dresser*, Bucke was doing more than making available Whitman's unpublished letters. Each collection may be seen as a gloss on a section of *Leaves of Grass*. *Calamus* provides an example of the 'adhesiveness' Whitman celebrated in the most controversial section of *Leaves of Grass* and testifies to the wholesomeness of Whitman's 'dear love of comrades'. In *The Wound Dresser* we see how he placed this love at the service of his country, and we follow him as he executes the daily tasks celebrated in *Drum-Taps*.

Unlike these two collections, which were addressed to the general reader, *Notes and Fragments*[10] was edited for the Whitman specialist. The work was privately printed, and Bucke solicited subscriptions by mailing a circular,[11] but the response was disheartening. On 2 May 1899 Bucke wrote to Traubel: '—I note what you say about printing "Notes & Fragments" [in the] East and have no doubt you are right, in the mean time, however, it is quite doubtful whether the book will be printed at all as the Whitman men do not seem to crave for it to any alarming extent.'[12] However, a few days later, on 9 May, Bucke had decided to print the book: 'Subscriptions for "Notes & Fragments" have about ceased to come in, though I may get some from England. I have not yet enough money to pay for printing, but I hope to bring the book out somehow.'[13] On 11 May he issued another circular to the subscribers: 'I have not enough subscriptions to cover the cost of producing the book, nevertheless, I shall begin printing next week and will issue copies as soon as possible. Shall limit the issue to 200 copies and shall number each.'[14] *Notes and Fragments* was printed that year, in London, Ontario, for private distribution, in an edition of 225 copies.[15]

The Complete Writings of Walt Whitman,[16] issued under the editorial supervision of the literary executors in 1902, includes Bucke's editions of *The Wound Dresser, Calamus,* and *Notes and Fragments,* along with all Whitman's publishing writings. The only new materials prepared for this edition were Oscar Lovell Trigg's variorum readings of *Leaves of Grass* and his Whitman bibliography. Bucke died before the work was published.

(25)

To William D. O'Connor

[?] June '88

My dear O'Connor

Of course no one will want you to subscribe—indeed you must not—but it would not be right not to let you know what is going on and the best way to do this is to send the circular.[1] I have your letter of 6th was very glad to get it, shall answer it soon at present over eyes & ears in work (after my absence). I think W. W. will be as well now (for a time at least) as he has been lately—he was a very sick man

R M Bucke

[1]Included with the letter is a printed text of the circular, marked *'Copy proof'* (Feinberg: LC):

"What you give me I cheerfully accept.
A little sustenance, a hut and garden, a little money, as I rendezvous with my poems,
A traveler's lodging and breakfast as I journey through the States—why should I be ashamed to own such gifts? Why to advertise for them?
For I myself am not one who bestows nothing upon man and woman,
For I bestow upon any man or woman the entrance to all the gifts of the universe."

—*L. of G.*

It is pretty generally known that WALT WHITMAN has not now and has never had any money. What he has earned in the course of his life, by writing and otherwise, he has always used for the benefit of others, after subtracting from it enough to purchase for himself the bare necessities of life. For many years he has lived in the most frugal manner in a little house in Camden, alone with his kind and excellent housekeeper, Mrs. Davis, but the time has come when it is no longer possible for him to go on in this way, his growing feebleness (from age and paralysis) has reached a point (especially since his recent illness) at which he is no longer able to care suitably for himself, nor is it proper that he should any longer be left alone at night. This being the case certain of his friends have engaged a man (half nurse, half servant) who will always be within call and will assist and care for the good gray poet. It will be necessary to retain this man at an expense of perhaps $600 a year as long as Mr. Whitman lives, and his friends are asked to contribute for this purpose. Should the contributions warrant it, other additions to the comfort of his surroundings will be made.

A certain amount will be raised at once, when that is gone more will be asked for, and so on as long as it is needed.

No one is asked to give—it is taken for granted that those who know the venerable poet, either personally or through his works, will be glad to subscribe.

Those to whom this circular is sent are asked not only to contribute something themselves, but to send either Mr. Harned, Mr. Donaldson, or Dr. Bucke the name and address of any person known to them who would probably be glad to assist. Those to whom more than one copy of the circular is sent are asked to distribute these in their turn, and should they want more they may send to any of the three persons above mentioned for them.

The following sums have already been subscribed, and from time to time new editions of this circular will be issued giving the names of all subscribers down to date.

R. M. Bucke, $25.00
Thomas Harned,
Thomas Donaldson,
   Money should be sent, by registered letter, cheque, or post office order, to one of the three persons named below, who will be responsible for the care and proper expenditure thereof, viz:—

THOMAS DONALDSON	THOMAS HARNED	DR. R. M. BUCKE
Attorney-at-Law	*Counsellor-at-Law*	Asylum
316 N. 40th Street	Federal Street	London, Ont.,
Philadelphia, Penn.	Camden, New Jersey	Canada
18th June, 1888.		

Both Whitman and the other disciples disapproved of Bucke's circular. Traubel reports that 'W. was hot. Exclaimed: "I don't approve of it—I don't want the money—I have enough for all I need!" ' (Traubel, I, 349). On 19 July 1888, Bucke wrote Traubel that he had decided to abandon the circular (Feinberg: LC).

(26)

To Horace Traubel

[London, Ont.,] 2 July [188]8

I have (this morning) your two letters 29 & 30 June and one from W. W. of 29. [—] I feel much relieved that the will matter[1] is settled but I feel a deadly sinking when I look ahead at what is before us (but say nothing of this to any one, I would not say it to any but you but we are in the same boat and must sink or swim together) but we must brace up and go through with it—millions of eyes in the future will watch our actions today. Yes I have no doubt you are right and have seen clearer even than Osler (good doctor though he is), I fear Walt *cannot* rally, it is a steady gradual failing—with only *one* end in sight. But after that? It cannot be, surely it is simply impossible that that great spirit can go out like a candle? But even supposing he does might not anyone be content to die leaving behind him the imperishable renown that will follow our friend through all the ages? [—] Yes, it is clear to me that Osler *now* sees the end coming. I do not distrust your vigilance, not in the least but I cannot help worring and urging you, it seems to relieve me a little to do so. He should not leave his room upstairs *at present,* and he ought not to do any brain work[2] though I do not think *any thing* will affect the issue materially

R M Bucke

[1]On 3 and 4 June Whitman suffered three strokes. By chance Bucke, who was on a business trip, stopped to visit him on the 3d and thus could act as his physician in this crisis. He decided that Whitman must make a will, and Harned drafted one. On 29 June Whitman wrote Bucke: 'I have finished & formally signed & witnessed the *will & testimentary matters complete*—including the dispensating of copyrights & literary matters by a sort of trustee-board, yourself, Harned & Horace Traubel—' (WW 1729). The daily events of this crucial period and the details of the will are reported in great detail in Traubel, I, 254–306, 310–12.
[2]Whitman was completing *November Boughs.*

(27)

To Horace Traubel

[London, Ont.,] 9 July [188]8

I have your letters of 6th & 7th and W's of 5th & 6th. [—]
About Donaldson, I do not understand his apparent avoid-
ance of his pressing responsibility but I do not believe he
has abandoned us, think you will find him in the right
place yet.[1] [—] You or Harned or both must see him and
get from himself what his position is to be. I expect he is
driven with other engagements and perhaps waiting to see
certain parties before reporting. Meantime Harned himself
has never said a word about the circular, whether to drop it
or not & if so what to do without it. We certainly ought to
have money both for W. now & while he is with us and for
the funeral. I wish you & Harned would write me your full
ideas on this money question, but before we actually settle
anything about it H. should *see* D. and get his views, it
may be that D. has already collected a certain sum—he sent
messages w̄h seemed to mean that or something like it. [—]
Next about the funeral itself [/] I will write Burroughs today, he ought to do it—is the right man—(I not being a
native American am certainly not the right man /though I
would far rather do my best than have it said W's friends
had not a word to say for him when he came to be buried/).
If O'Connor was not sick he would stand next to B. If B.
will not act I am in favor of asking Col. Robt. Ingersol—this
nonsense abt. his atheism amounts to nothing—he is really
one of the most religious men living[2]—Knows W. & likes
him. About conducting the funeral in silence I can never
consent to that—to take a last leave of such a man without
a farewell would be clownish, unworthy. Again about
singing and reading we must absolutely avoid every thing
like theatricallity—I think we should be on the safest
ground (and we must avoid sneers and criticism as much
for his sake as our own) to swiftly meet at the grave, have
some one speak for 10, 15, or 20 minutes—then lower
down the coffin and cover it in silence. You H & I[,] I

suppose[,] will have to settle this matter at last—let us not leave it to the last—if we do we shall have more than we can carry. And mind this whoever is to speak must have a little while to prepare. Do you & H put your heads together & think your best what is *best* to do. Write me again— meanwhile I will have an answer from B. if possible. (I would not say positively that it would not be well to have the Death Carol sung by a really good voice—I would like to leave this open for consideration and it might be as well to have the matter in some kind of shape in case of need). I think this is all for today.

By the way I am not too sure that *besides the address* it would not be well to have (perhaps by H[s] clergiman friend, or another) during the lowering of the coffin &c certain Psalms (say picked verses of 39th & 90th) and perhaps some verses from the New Testament recited

But think it all over and let me know your conclusions

Your friend
R M Bucke

[1]Thomas Donaldson had plans to appeal to Whitman's English friends for funds. On 17 July 1888 Bucke wrote Traubel: 'No, I do not like Donaldson's course at all, from any point of view. . . . I do not like this appeal to England and passing by American friends' (Feinberg: LC).
[2]Colonel Robert Green Ingersoll, a politician and noted lecturer, was known to his contemporaries as 'the great agnostic'.

(28)
To Walt Whitman

[London, Ont.,] 11 July [188]8
I was greatly pleased today to get your card of 9th [.] I heard too from Traubel and Harned. Harned enclosed a mem. from Donaldson. All seems to be going well *around* you, I wish all was going as well with you—as indeed probably *it is*, although I fear in the meantime you are uncomfortable, even suffering. Would it not be as well, Walt, to sell the horse—Harned could attend to it—it will

be full as cheap to hire by & by when you want to go out—if that time comes. As the matter stands the horse is eating her head off and taking harm from want of exercise.[1]

I am sorry to hear that Baker[2] is about to leave you but perhaps the next man will be as good. I am glad to think you are well enough to get on without a regular nurse but however well you get you must always henceforth have a man to help & take care of you

Your friend
R M Bucke

[1]After writing to Whitman, Bucke wrote to Traubel: 'I wrote W. yesterday advising him to sell horse & buggy & *hire* when better—I do not see how he *can* get better' (Feinberg: LC). Whitman perceived the real reason for Bucke's advice: he mentioned to Traubel that 'in Doctor's opinion I am never to find much use for them again' (Traubel, I, 464).
[2]Dr. Nathan M. Baker.

(29)

To Horace Traubel

[London, Ont.,] 13 July [188]8

My dear Horace

I have your two letters of 11th. I have not heard from Burroughs. I have a scheme for the funeral which I want you to talk over with Harned. Very roughly it is as follows: can of course be modified as thought well:

1 A short address by Burroughs

2 Have O'Connor read pp 39–43 of his "Good Gray Poet"

3 Clifford[1] to recite some passages from the psalms and perhaps from L of G. as well & from New Testament perhaps as the body is being lowered into the grave

4 Then I would speak for perhaps 20 or 25 minutes
The whole service to be afterwards printed in a little pamphlet and sold and distributed as widely as possible.

5 The singing of the death carol might also come in. Talk all this over with Harned and if you & he see good lay it before Clifford personally (or by letter if he has gone). Let

me know what the verdict is—we must positively be ready for whatever may come—I know well that as far as I am concerned I could *do nothing* at the last minute unless it was all arranged & ready beforehand

Your friend

R M Bucke

[1] The Rev. John Herbert Clifford, a minister of the Unitarian Church in Germantown, Pennsylvania, and a friend of Whitman and Traubel.

(30)

To Horace Traubel

[London, Ont.,] 15th July [188]8

My dear Horace

I have heard from Burroughs, he says it would be *impossible* for him to act so I suppose that must be given up. I enclose a letter to O'Connor w̄h you will /first read, carefully and then/ mail or not as you think best after consulting with Harned—If you & he think my programe (or something like it) should be carried out of course you will send it.—In any case you have now my ideas and know what I am myself prepared to do and I leave the matter in your hands to arrange all details and I hope you will not lose time in getting things into such shape that each one /may/ *know* what he is to do and be well *prepared* to do it. I have your very much valued letter of 12th [/] Poor Walt seems to me to be mighty sick and weak and miserable. It is hard, infernally hard, to see him suffer so; but we must just bear it and meantime stand to our guns and do what is to be done. [—] From a conversation Mr. Smith,[1] Mrs. Geo. Whitman,[2] Mrs Davis & myself had on 12th June I should judge the Whitmans' ideas on the funeral subject would correspond closely with our own. However, after getting our plans into some shape it might be as well for Harned to see Mr Geo. Whitman and have a definite understanding with him. Yes, Morse[3] would be a man we could use but

100

he is erratic and bad to depend upon I believe. If you do
not ask Col. I. or he cannot act (though I think he will) you
must try and find another man to speak at the opening—If
O'C. will not or cannot act I suppose he must just be left
out & that place be left vacant

R M Bucke

Keep me fully informed as to all funeral arrangements as
of all other matters

RMB

[1]Robert Pearsall Smith, a prominent Quaker minister and one of Whitman's closest Philadelphia friends.
[2]The wife of Whitman's younger brother, George Washington Whitman, with
whom Whitman lived (1873–84) before moving to his own house on Mickle
Street.
[3]Sidney H. Morse, American sculptor. His bust of Whitman is reproduced in
Corr., IV, following p. 278.

(31)

To Horace Traubel

[London, Ont.,] 21 July [188]8

My dear Horace

I enclose a note from O'Connor just received—*I want you
to return it to me.* [—] I wrote O'C. that certainly we would
leave the thing open but trusted he would be there. I suggested that he might *speak by a substitute*, provided the
words were his—If he *wrote* them for instance and some one
else read them—then he might be *present* if possible but
even *that* would not be absolutely necessary. [—] I suppose
the music of the Burial Hymn that Cauffman will sing is
Sanford Villiers?[1] is it not? I have his music and could send
it you for Cauffman if he would like to have it—let me
know. I think we may count on O'C. if *he is above ground,*
he is in earnest and will come if the thing is in the cards. If
we could only get Ingersoll now I think we should be all
right. I do wish we could have had Burroughs if only for a
five minute address. But I suppose it is no use wishing, I

101

hear nothing further from him. Do you? Meanwhile W. seems to keep abt. the same but his life hangs on a thread. It seems certain that he cannot gain strength—that being so the first serious reverse (which may occur any day and *must* occur *soon*) will most likely end the struggle and we are at once face to face with the supreme crisis of our lives! I thought you & H knew abt. "Laurel Hill Cemetery" [/] R. P. Smith is anxious W. shd. be buried there and W. consented to it. So did Mrs Geo Whitman & G. W. It was all arranged before I left Phil[a] last time. I do not see that the *place* matters much so it is accessible, and will be kept in order (as it will be in L. H. C.) If neither Brooklin or N. Y. *claim* him it is not for us to look after *their* interests. W is *American* and *anywhere in America* would be a suitable place for his remains to rest. I am in favor of L. H. C. but if you like to arrange something else it will not signify to me. I should not like Camden—it is not the place. As for W[s] mother her remains could be moved to L. H. to rest by him—I think they should lie together. [—] As you remark W[s] hand writing is failing, getting uncertain still it is wonderfull how good on the whole it keeps—he might go on some little time but I do not believe he will be with us when the leaves fall. Some little thing will almost certainly occur to break the worn thread by which he holds to life within the next two or three months. I should think a real hot spell, such as you are sure to have in the next eight weeks, would be very trying for him.

I think I have touched on every thing down to date. I hope you & H. will keep moving in the matter of arranging for the funeral—If any thing is left undone at the last it will be bad.

Goodly by the moment

Your friend
R M Bucke

[1]Charles Villiers Stanford, *Elegiac Ode: The Words from President Lincoln's Burial Hymn by Walt Whitman* (New York, 1884).

(32)

To Horace Traubel

[London, Ont.,] 29 July [188]8

Yours of 26th came to hand yesterday. I am glad to see the Ingersoll slip and have good hopes now that he will fall in with our views. [—] In re advising W. W. to sell his horse, leave off work &c. &c. I guess we had better drop it altogether, he never did and he never will "take advice" and to tell the truth I do not think men who amount to anything ever do. I agree with you that it would be better that he should drop work but this opinion rests on the supposition that we know his business better than he does and possibly that it is not strictly true. It is just possible that the old man may know more about his business than even we do. One thing I see plainly—he is determined to leave a record of himself with his own hand to the very end if possible—You are likely to have some hot weather now I should think, I should fear that great heat, especially if continued for weeks, would affect W. unfavorably and it is certain he cannot stand much of a put down without going altogether

Your friend
R M Bucke

(33)

To Horace Traubel

[London, Ont.,] 5 August [188]8

My dear Horace

I have yours of 2[d], I think you deserve the greatest praise for the way you are sticking to poor old Walt and his fortunes at this crisis. I wish I could help you bear some of the load but do not see how. I wonder what D[onaldson]. is doing? Anything? And H[arned]. does not seem to be very lively, I do not know any one in this part of the country who I could ask for a monthly sum—no doubt with the circular I might have got a few 5 & 10 dollar bills—Then I know I could have got money from England but I do not like to apply there for it unless it should seem necessary. It mades me mad sometimes, as mad as damnation to see the Americans so apathetic about by far the greatest man the country has so far produced but it is no use—we must just keep cool—I guess in the end you will get the subsidy you want and a few months will probably relieve the country of the burden—many an American in the future will blush for the apathy of his ancestors today![1]

Your friend
R M Bucke

[1]Since Bucke's scheme for raising money for Whitman by means of a circular had been abandoned and Donaldson's efforts did not seem to produce results, Traubel decided to initiate a subscription fund. In his entry for 10 August 1888, he noted: 'I have started a Whitman fund—am trying to get a small monthly guarantee each from a group of people to pay for the nurse and extras required by W.s persistent illness. W. does not know anything about the fund. I have not explained anything to him in detail. Hard to find friends, however' (Traubel, II, 116).

(34)

To Horace Traubel

[London, Ont.,] 6 Aug [188]8

My dear Horace

I have your two letters of 3^d [/] I do not believe you get all my letters [/] At all events you do not notice them—I wrote asking whether you would have $25. or $3. a month [/] However I shall send $3. a month, put me down for that, will mail you tomorrow the payment for 1 July & 1 Aug. and will send each month after this—the P. S. orders will be made payable to H[arned]. I have a note from Johnston, he tells me he has sent $25. I will send the same amount or double if wanted every quarter. [—] I think you will get the guarantees you want if you just stick to it awhile—if I see a chance to help you I will chip in. [—] I am surprised that Williams[1] should have made to you the statement you quote. There is not a word of truth in it.

104

W. W. is paying the penalty of nursing the sick soldiers in the hospitals and of his intense sympathy for them while sick & wounded. I do not believe (& I think I know something about it) that Walt ever committed any excess of any kind—he has lived a free joyous life and taken his share of the pleasures of life but never in such a way as to be injured thereby. There is no relation whatever between the disease of which he is slowly dying and excess of any kind.

I am greatly surprised often that so many of W^s friends, sensible people too apparently, should [have] misinterpreted the "Ch^n of Adam" poems as they do. Think that they admit excess in the author and allow or encourage it in others. [—] The poems have always seemed to me strong evidence of purity in the man who wrote them and strong incentive to purity in the readers of them

Your friend
R M Bucke

¹Talcott Williams, a friend of Whitman's and editor of the Philadelphia *Press*.

(35)

To Horace Traubel

[London, Ont.,] 9 Aug [188]8

My dear Horace

I have just read with great interest your letter of 7th. No doubt your experience with the fund is somewhat trying but you ought not to be discouraged—consider if you were trying to raise such a fund for any *other writer?* By the time you get through you will have a pretty good idea "how much fame goes to $1.?" You might write a good magazine article on that subject, might you not? How many of Tennyson's readers would subscribe money for him? There is one good thing we shall know by the time we get through /viz:/ who are our friends & who not—If necessary of course I will increase my subscription to any reasonable required amount. I would rather suffer myself or even see my family suffer than that W. should—but it does not follow from that that I should chip in and do what other[s] ought to do. I have in the last ten years invested I dare say $1500. in this W. W. business and am prepared to invest as much more *if necessary.*— I am very glad you have made up your mind to remain at Camden, do not see what we should do without you there. What you say about Wˢ present physical condition touches me much closer than the fund matter [/] I greatly fear we shall not need the latter for long, he *cannot* surely go on in this way a great while. We *know* that real gain is impossible [/] *Any* change *must* be for the worse and there is no stability about his present state. I am glad to hear that the rest of the sheets will be here soon—I was intensely interested in the *Hospital* piece,[1] and am ever more anxious to see the Hicks piece.[2] [—] Marvin[3] I think is quite poor but I do not know his financial position accurately—there are doubtless any number of people who would give if they knew—would not Col. Ingersoll? he has plenty of money. If money is not needed (the fund being guaranteed) there would be no objict in a $5. autograph ed. of the book—but if we had not raised the money I should have advised (as W. & I planned long ago) a $10. book ("L of G." "Sp. Days" & "A.B."[4] bount in one, on large paper well bound, autograph, good many pictures) for private sale. If W. should ever (which he won't) make any sort of rally, should like to see that scheme carried out yet

Your friend
R M Bucke

[1]'Last of the War Cases', *November Boughs,* pp. 109–17.
[2]'Notes (Such As They Are) Founded on Elias Hicks', *ibid.,* pp. 119–40.
[3]Joseph B. Marvin, a friend of Whitman's, worked for the Treasury in Washington.
[4]He means "N.B." or *November Boughs.*

(36)

To Horace Traubel

[London, Ont.,] 30 Aug [188]8

My dear Horace

I have yours of 28th[.] Your acct. of Wˢ condition is pretty discouraging but I do not suppose you could truthfully give a better one. I feel satisfied that the end is drawing near and am satisfied now that he should die, if only greater, more absolute paralisis, greater mental collapse, dementia, can be avoided. It is bad enough to have W. die but how infinitely worse it would be to have him live on his mind gone—a blank. That would be terrible—however I do not anticipate anything so terrible—I do not believe he will live to pass into that state. You speak of a rally. I do not believe any real rally is possible [/] it is just a question of how long he can live at the present rate of decline. But over and above that there is the extreme possibility of a sudden end from brain change which may take place at almost any moment. I can well understand how you feel about all this—constantly with him as you are—it is hard on you now but by and by you will be glad enough that it was your priviledge to be so intimately connected with our friend in his last days. I have a copy of frontispiece and like it fairly well—it should not be used *alone* except perhaps in "N. B." but will probably be a standard picture in the future to use along with earlier ones—considered just as a picture (although rough) I think it good and as a likeness it is fair. I will do what I can with W. about the book ("N. B." & "C. W."¹) but do not fancy I can make him alter any plan he may have in his head—I fully endorse all you say about the advisability of having the book issued by W. himself to the purchaser—think it would give an additional value to the book and be an inducement to many to buy. I do not understand why this Ingersoll matter is not attended to. One comfort O'Connor (I had a letter from him yesterday) is fully alive to the importance of the occasion and will be

with us if he can move—If now O'C. was able to speak &
Burroughs to be there, even if silent, I should not care so
much abt Ingersoll. We could get on.

Your friend
R M Bucke

[1]Complete Works, i.e., *Complete Poems & Prose, 1855–1888.*

(37)

To Horace Traubel

[London, Ont.,] 8 Sept [188]8

Private

My dear Horace

I have yours of 6th [—] About Gilchrist and the meaning
of his visit here—I do not know—but I was told a year
ago that the last time he was in America he had a com-
mission from some English friends of W. W. to try and
arrange for W. literary executorship to be located in
England—I was told that he actually made a proposition of
this kind to W. which was met with some hauteur—
almost indignation—I think perhaps no such proposition
was ever made but have no means of arriving at certainty.
I have a strong suspicion that H. G.[s] present visit is made
partly at least to be on the spot when W. dies—no doubt
he would wish to be near him—but also he may think of
other possible advantages to himself, friends or country.
The English people realize the intense interest with [sic]
will attach to any *personal* remains of W. more than we do
perhaps. They see less of W. and there is more halo of
romance about him. I find no fault with H. G.[s] ambition—
it is natural and springs from his admiration of W. but *we*
must think of America and the American friends first. I
hope G. will not try to be about W. more than is good for
W. Keep me posted on this point. It is quite possible that
G. is the agent of English friends of W. to see how W. is

situated in his illness and that everything possible is done for him—this would no doubt be a part of the programe—but I do not doubt that the other or something like it is also an important part of it. You will of course keep your eyes open and will see that *no one* comes between W. and you—you of course meaning *us three* and us three meaning *America.* You may show this if you like to Harned *but to no one else.*[1] [—] Tell me how you stand with *Marvin, Gilder* and *Harkness* when you write next. [—] Your subsidy must be (with Ingersoll) nearly enough is it not? But I suppose you could use a little more than $60 a month could you not? [—] Have you seen my notes to W. declining the Horse and phaeton? Was W. at all vexed that I did so? Of course I would take them if wanted but there would be no sense in it[2]

Your friend
R M Bucke

[1]A few days later Bucke reconsidered his suspicions about possible infiltration by the British. On 14 September 1888, he wrote Traubel: 'On returning home today found three letters from you of 10th 11th & 12th. Gilchrist's movements, especially in view of the fact that he does not seem particularly bent on seeing W. are highly mysterious—possibly there is some private reason for his reappearance in this country. A young woman? Get some woman to look into this! Poor G. seems to be somewhat lost in the inane' (Feinberg: LC).
[2]On 2 September 1888, Whitman offered to give Bucke his mare and phaeton as a payment for a debt of two hundred dollars (WW 1779). Two days later Bucke responded: 'I do not consider that you owe me anything (the balance is the other way) . . . I think you ought to have Harned or Traubel see to selling the horse & wagon there and use the money to hire an easy carriage whenever you are able to get out for a drive' (Feinberg: LC).

(38)

To Walt Whitman

10 Sept [188]8

How do the fates serve you these last few lovely days? Well I hope. We are all well here and the meter goes on quietly and well as far as we know. Nothing fresh however. The autumn weather here is just perfect, sunshiny, dreamy.

Puts one in mind all the time of Tennyson's "Lotus Eaters". How goes the book—I hope to get a perfect autograph copy of both N. B. & C. W.[1] from you before a very great while—I shall look upon them as the crown and summit of all my W. W. collection—a collection by the way which gives me a lot of worry sometimes to think what I am eventually to do with it.[2] I regard it as so precious that no ordinary disposition of it will do—I am sorry to hear that Kennedy's book is not to be out at present—I fear it is quite a disappointment to him.[3]

I am going to write an elaborate annual report this year mostly on "Alcohol" am in the middle of it—expect to give the alcohol men a "black eye"[4]

Affectionately yours
R M Bucke

---

[1]*November Boughs* and *Complete Poems & Prose, 1855–1888.*
[2]He left the collection to his children, who put it up at auction in England; see *Catalogue of . . . Walt Whitman: The Property of . . . Dr. Richard Maurice Bucke* (London, 1935).
[3]William Sloane Kennedy's book was eventually published as *Reminiscenses of Walt Whitman* (London, 1896).
[4]Bucke forbad the use of beer, wine, or alcohol in any form in his asylum, a significant reform (Coyne, p. 36).

(39)

To Walt Whitman

[London, Ont.,] 28 Sept [188]8

I have your good letter of 25 & 26 inst. I note all you say about my "W. W." Your wishes will be religiously respected [/] I did think of considerable changes (for I am certain the book will sell by & by) but was *never* set on them and less so lately. Yes, I shall leave it stand as it is and add under a later date what else I may have to say.[1] I am glad D^r. Osler has been to see you again, I do not think the pain you speak of means anything serious, though no doubt it is annoying—I hope it is gone by now. Have to go to go [sic] to the city in a few minutes shall take this in and post it [;] some men (capitalists) coming this afternoon to see the meter [,] shall tell you tomorrow whether we succeed in doing any business with them. We are moving slow just now—we hope to be in a position soon to launch out[2]

Your friend
R M Bucke

[1]On 25 September Whitman advised Bucke not to make any changes in the biography (WW 1799).
[2]Bucke hoped to make his fortune—and that of several others, including Horace Traubel and Alfred Forman—on a gas and water meter invented by his brother-in-law, William John Gurd. Nothing ever came of the scheme, and Whitman's attitude toward Bucke's speculations fluctuated between indifference and exasperation.

(40)

To Walt Whitman

[London, Ont.,] 24 Oct [188]8

I have heard from Wm Gurd. All goes well in N. Y. except that our lawyer has just been sick, he is better and the work of taking out the patents will go on now with all convenient speed. Cannot tell *yet* when I shall positively go East but rather expect sometime this week. [—] There is no doubt Dr Osler thinks you are doing well or he would be over oftener, if he thought of you failing or very ill he would not neglect you I am sure. He is an exceptionally able man and we must admit (whatever we may think or feel) that he knows as much about your condition as any one does (including yourself).[1] I do not hear good accounts of your present nurse (Musgrove) and I have just written to Horace about a young man whom I can freely recommend who is willing to go from here and take the place. His name is Edward Wilkins, I know you would like him[/] he is a real good, nice looking, young fellow, I have known him some years—he is as good as he looks.[2] I expect to hear from Horace at once on this business—I hope you will approve of the change, I am sure you will be pleased with it when made,

Affectionately yours

R M Bucke

[1]On 1 October 1888, Bucke reported that he had written to Osler for a diagnosis of Whitman's condition; on 3 October 1888, he quoted from Osler's reply: 'He [Osler] says he finds you "decidedly better", "brighter mentally and physically holding your own", "the pain" he says "points to nothing serious" ' (Feinberg: LC). Whitman and Traubel discussed Osler's diagnosis as reported by Bucke: 'W. said: "I confess I do not wholly like or credit what he says—I do not fancy the jaunty way in which he seems inclined to dismiss the troubles. Still, that may all be a part of his settled policy—I do not object to cheer. I don't know whether it's from getting down to hard pan or is a theory, but, whatever, Osler pursues it, and it is right—it is inspiring. Still, I know my condition—don't need him to tell me about that—can't be fooled" ' (Traubel, II, 432).
[2]At this time, Edward Wilkins was a night attendant in the infirmary at the London Asylum (*Corr.*, IV, 117n).

(41)

To Horace Traubel

[London, Ont.,] 6 Nov [188]8

My dear Horace

Nothing further from Wm Gurd but I look each mail now for a letter fixing the date of our meeting in N. Y. The next thing will be leave of absence. Card from W. today he says "Edward Wilkins has arrived here all safely & is welcome." I hope to hear from *you* about E. W. tomorrow. Your letter of 5th (just to hand) proposing an address from me in C[lifford]'s church is rather a staggerer—I do not altogether dislike the idea—but what about the congregation? I have my doubts how it might strike *them*—another thing—I have counted on hearing C. speak and certainly I will not consent to any thing that prevents this. We must let it stand—I will think it over & see if I can find any thing to say. [—] How would an argumentative address on immortality from the point of view of evolution strike you? Showing that the lower the mind (the further back we go) the

112

less the faith in I[mmortality]. & vice versa the higher the mind (especially the moral nature) the greater (stronger) the f[aith]. in I.—that finally in the latest & highest mind (W. W.) the faith is deeper & stronger than ever before. &c &c &c &c it is a big subject & would take abt 3/4 hour to do any thing with it—guess that would be too long?[1] [—] However I will think it over & we will talk it over—meantime nothing must be considered settled. I may be two Sundays in Phil[a]—I shall certainly insist on hearing C. the *first* Sunday I am there. [—] I judge W. W. gets on fairly well—wish I could infer as much in re O'C. Nothing new here

Good luck to you!
R M Bucke

[1]Apparently this address, to the congregation of the Rev. John Herbert Clifford's Unitarian Church in Germantown, Pennsylvania, was to be a summary of the thesis of *Man's Moral Nature*. Whitman was enthusiastic: 'That would make Clifford's church the church of churches: I am doubtful about my figuring in it: as for the rest, it seems both proper and wise. That is Doctor's thunder anyway: the evolution of the race from low to high, good to better, slowly, slowly, inevitably: Bucke is primed—full to the brim: can sit down by the hour anytime—talk the best talk about big things. Now, keep at him: don't let him evade you' (Traubel, III, 68).

(42)

To Horace Traubel

[London, Ont.,] 9 Nov [188]8

My dear Horace

I had today yours of 7th, a long letter from W. of 6th & 7th, a note from Gurd, & a P. C. from Burroughs. The latter is going from home for a week or more and hopes I shall not go East untill he gets back. Gurd has nothing to tell, patents not yet fixed but he expects from day to day to send for me—otherwise (except for delay) all O. K. [—] W. writes very cheerfully speaks of feeling "better still". He seems to like Ed. Wilkins well as I was sure he would. I do not believe the "Clifford idea" as you call it can come to

113

any thing—I would not like to do such a thing unless I felt I could do it well. [—] At present I am overloaded [/] have neither time nor force to put into any new thing. [—] If only the meter would succeed (as I know it ought to) then indeed! But now with both meter and asylum on my back over and above the ordinary cares and worries of a man with a big family—I tell you I have got my load! But the temptation to say something about W. is with me the greatest of all temptations, we shall see, we shall see—but meanwhile count on nothing

Your friend
R M Bucke

Should this meter *go* it is my dream to devote the rest of my life (not many years perhaps, but still a few) to the study and promulgation of the new religion ("The great idea") and I should hope to find younger men to pass on the work to when I laid it down

R M Bucke

(43)

To Walt Whitman

[London, Ont.,] 22 Nov [188]8

If I had Hamlin Garland's address I think I would write him a few lines to say how much I admire his calm and pleasant sentences in the "Transcript".[1] I do not know when I have read any think that pleased me more—not I think since I read O'Connor's letter in the N. Y. Tribune on the Osgood-Stevens affair.[2] We are coming to the front at last—and shall come—I have no fear, no doubt. It is only a question of waiting a few years untill men have time to take it in. Another quarter or half century will see L. of G. acknowledged to be what it really is—The bible of America. [—] My visit East is likely to be delayed some weeks. We have abt. decided that we will not show the meter untill it is protected (by patent) in other countries as well as in the States. Wm Gurd will return here from N. Y.

114

almost at once and proceed to Ottawa—arrange there for the Canadian and other patents—as soon as these are secured we shall go East. I, of course, cannot say how soon this will be but I am in hopes we shall get to Phil[a] immediately after Xmas. [—] Saw Pardee[3] on monday [/] he is bad—very sick indeed—mind very feeble. Do not hear from O'Connor, do you? [—] I am thinking over something to say about you and L. of G. if I have the chance when I am in Phil[a]; impossible to say yet what it will come to, if anything.—must only wait and see. It seems to me a long time since I wrote you last—I have been in a kind of whirl, better luck in future!

Love to you
R M Bucke

[1]Garland's review of *November Boughs* appeared in the Boston *Transcript* of 15 November 1888.
[2]See Bucke's letter to Whitman of 9 May 1882.
[3]The Honorable Timothy Blair Pardee, a close friend of Bucke's, was politically prominent in Ontario.

(44)

To Walt Whitman

[London, Ont.,] 3 Dec [188]8

Your letter of Friday & Saturday (30th & 1st) came to hand this afternoon and has made me feel very anxious for you. I fear you are suffering a great deal. I have written to Osler urging him to try and do something to relieve that horrible irritation of the bladder that keeps you getting up so much at night and it seems to me imperative that the bowels should be kept open.[1] I fear Osler is too busy to give you the attention you require and it seems to me that you ought to have him recommend a good man who would see you every day, and twice a day if necessary while O. himself would come over from time to time and see you with him. I have also written to Traubel urging him to make some arrangement by which you will be seen at least once a day by some good doctor—I wish I could be with you but that is impossible at present. I shall hope to hear very soon that proper arrangements have been made and that you are more comfortable

I am always

Affectionately yours
R M Bucke

---

[1]The same day Bucke wrote to Traubel: 'W. cannot possibly go on as at present [/] *he cannot live so*—it seems he is very constipated and suffers greatly with irritation of the bladder so much that he was up friday night "40 to 50 times" ' (Feinberg: LC).

(45)

To Horace Traubel

[London, Ont.,] 14 Dec [188]8

My dear Horace

I have yours of 12th [—] W. must have rallied surely or I should have a had a telegram by this? I understand perfectly that he is very low and that the end might come almost any day. I shall *answer* any telegram at once so do not feel *sure* I have it untill you get answer. Yes I want *very much* to be with you for a couple of days before the end if that could be—but it will be difficult, very likely impossible to see so far ahead and for me to go East on a false alarm would be most disastrous in the present juncture of affairs, that *must* be avoided. If the thing was possible I would go East almost at once and wait for the end (unless a marked change for the better should take place, which is not to be looked for.) [—] It was arranged between us that I should call on Burroughs on my way East—some weeks ago however he wrote me that he should be from home for a time—he has not notified me of his return, seems as if he was not anxious to see me. We must not do anything (unless some necessary thing) that would really hurt the feelings of any of W[s] friends, that would be certainly *wrong*, but as to what is *right* I do not at present see my way—we must wait till the time comes to settle details—I am beginning to think that for the sake of peace we shall have to have a silent funeral—nobody would want to speak with half the company desiring silence—and certainly we do not want to keep W^s friends from his funeral—there would be *other* times and places to speak when we all wd desire to listen. We might summon a meeting of W^s friends *immediately* after his death and settle the matter then

R M B

(46)

To Horace Traubel

[London, Ont.,] 16 Dec [188]8

My dear Horace

I cannot get this funeral business out of my head and cannot see my way to a solution of the difficulty.

To take the body of W. W. to the grave, bury and come away as if we had buried a criminal or an animal and were on the whole a little ashamed of the transaction!

To have some clergiman read his verses and say his prayers over the grave and stultify W^s whole life and our convictions and professions.

How can we accept either of these? I think I would rather stay here and ignore the whole business. But how can I do that? I could never hold my head up again and I believe I should actually die within a very few years of pure shame.

On the other hand to arrange a ceremony with reading, singing and speaking (as per "Bucke's program") and carry it out with half of those present feeling hurt and disgusted, what remidy is this?

For God's sake let us see our way to something definite.

We ought to by rights (and must) know the views of enough of W^s friends to sustain us in the cause adopted. If I could do it I would see a number of them. But could not H. & yourself see several about Phil^a & Camden?

117

If nothing definite is settled before Wˢ death I would suggest that immediately upon death taking place H. should ask say a dozen or twenty (you might make a list and have it ready) of Wˢ most prominent friends (including of course B[urroughs].) from Phila. N. Y. &c &c to his house and let the matter be settled then and there (that would be say the day before the funeral so that those from a distance could stay over for the funeral). Or would it be better that we three (as executors) after consulting George and Jefferson W.[1] (they must in any case be consulted) take the matter into our hands? (We should have the power and right.) If *this* is settled upon George & Jefferson might be consulted at once—George in person and he (if he could not answer for Jeff.) might write J.

Talk this over with H. and see if you cannot do something towards a settlement. Advise me.

I wish you had said what Talcott Williams seemed to think of the business. You said B. had written him but not what W. thought.

If we should settle, before the end, just what was to be done the program might be given on the printed funeral notices, then those who did not like it could stay away.

I fear it is hopeless in any case to look for unanimity—we must not figure on that. See H. and answer this letter freely & fully

R M Bucke

P. S. (An hour afterwards) I want to add that upon full consideration my own deliberate opinion is that we three (as executors, after all, we must shoulder the responsibility of what is done and if we consent to what we do not approve how should we answer it?) if we are unanimous (as I suppose we are) shᵈ act upon our conviction of what is right (as we are bound to do being executors). That we should see a very few of Wˢ most intimate friends (including his brothers) then settle upon what is to be done, arrange for it, announce it with the funeral notice and carry it out. [—] We are and must be responsible—let us be responsible for what we approve not for what any one else approves

R M Bucke

¹Whitman's brothers. George lived in Camden; Jefferson lived in St. Louis, Mo.

(47)

To Walt Whitman

[17 December 1888]

An impromptu criticism on the 900 page Volume, "The Complete Poems and Prose of Walt Whitman," first issued December, 1888.¹

* * * * It is grand, grander than even I had hoped. It is the bible of the future for the next thousand years, and after that (superseded by even greater poems) to live as a classic for ever. It is a gigantic massive autobiography, the first of its kind, (though the trick had been tried before by Goethe, Rousseau, and others; but even Goethe could not do it). The title-page is perfect—I cannot conceive anything finer—and the little notes (opening and closing) are (to my notion—though you seemed so doubtful about them) just right.

Dear Walt, you have had a hard fight and a long fight, but we may say of you to-day that you have won the battle. If you have fallen at the end, (though I trust even yet you may still have before you some good days), but even if you are to fall now, your fame is safe beyond all peradventure. Your work is well done; and here or elsewhere, (I do not know that it matters which—except for those you leave a little while behind you), you will live and be honored always. Yes, and loved always.

R. M. Bucke

¹The manuscript of this letter is lost. The text survives in two broadsides printed for Whitman and in Traubel, III, 397–98. This is the text of the second broadside. For further discussion of the textual history of this letter, see Artem Lozynsky, 'Whitman's *Complete Poems & Prose:* "Bible" or "Volume"?', *Walt Whitman Review*, 19 (March 1973), 28–31, 34.

(48)

To Walt Whitman

[London, Ont.,] 31 Dec [188]8

Goodly poor old 88! Hurra for 89!

This morning your post card of 28th[,] your letter (enclosing Kennedy's) of 29th and the "Springfield Rep^n" for all which thanks. [—] Yesterday I read over again (for the 3d 4th or 5th time) "A Backward Glance" and "Elias Hicks" and dipped into a lot of other old favorites in the big Volume. Superficial readers will not of course detect the fine oblique personal touches running every where, through every page of this wonderfull book—nor do I pretend that I see the last meanings every where—But I see alot! More than in any other writing—but the subtlety of much of it is wonderfull and when seen that very elusiveness gives it an extraordinary piquancy. Yes, I think you need not doubt that you have got in so much of yourself and contemporary America that, a 'cute man reading the "C. W." hundreds of years from now could reconstruct in his own mind both you and your time & land in a truer and more radical sense than any past time of even 50 or 100 years back can be reconstituted from any book in actual existence and this for many reasons but cheifly for the reason of the unique *vitality* and suggestiveness of L. of G. [—] Yes, I think you may trust me to know *something* of your book & you, I have not studied them this last twenty years for nothing! If I did not know you both and love you both there would be something wrong on the one side or the other—but I don't think there is much wrong!

Love to you
R M Bucke

(49)

To Horace Traubel

[London, Ont.,] 16 Jan [188]9

My dear Horace

I have yours of 14th this morning. All quiet. [—] Meter

120

jogging along towards a state of readiness. We shall certainly be ready to go East 4 Feb. unless our N. Y. lawyer delays us and I do not think he will. [—] It is wonderfull how W. keeps in week after week and month after month—but my dear fellow the end has got to come [/] we must keep that steadily before us else we shall be knocked useless when it does come. I look for a sudden break down some day when least expected. Of course you will repeat this to *no one*. We must make up our minds to lose W. what I pray for is that his mind may remain clear as at present to the end. If this be granted us we may bear what comes as we can. [—] But it seems as if I c^d not bear it if his mind failed. It is too terrible to think about. It is wonderfull how clear and serene his mental vision is at present.

All well here

Affectionately
R M Bucke

(50)

To Horace Traubel

[London, Ont.,] 3 Feb [188]9

My dear Horace

I have not written for a few day—no time—Meanwhile I have received yours of 28 & 31 ult. and a couple of letters from W. (the last one, 31st about as cheery as any for a long time "a suspicion of something like strength" he says). Wh is good to hear. I do not see *why* you do not "prepare a W. paper" there are few who could speak of him with more authority. You must (I suppose you *do*) lay yourself out to speak of him (especially his "Last days") after he is gone. You will have a lecture on this subject which will be of exceeding interest by and by. You must collect little traits, expressions, glimpses of manner &c &c &c. You will be able to make it intensely interesting to all who love (as so many will) the grand old prophet.

121

I am fully aware how trying the meter delays must be to you, they are also to me but I have so much else to think about that they do not worry me much. I fear the fire and its effects will put us off now another week.[1] I counted on going 11th as I think I told you but Gurd & myself now think it will not be prudent for me to ask for leave untill 18th but I really have some confidence that we will start then if not sooner. Gurd is working on the meter all day long every day. Has just about finished another slightly different from first [/] we were testing it last night—it is marvellously accurate[.] I am confident it would measure a million gallons to a pint & perhaps much closer and rate or current-pressure &c would not affect it at all

Your friend

R M Bucke

If meter does not set us up it is a curious thing

RMB

[1]There was a fire at the Asylum on the night of 15 January, with damages estimated at \$4,000 to \$5,000.

(51)

To Horace Traubel

[London, Ont.,] 6 Feb [188]9

My dear Horace

I have yours of 4th. I understand it (and *you*) thoroughly. If all is well with the meter you shall be placed in the position you naturally and properly desire. Such a company as we expect to found *must* have a book keeper (will perhaps have a *staff* of them after a little)[.] You must have that place and I trust if it comes to a *staff* you will be the head of it. There is nothing new (of any kind) to write since yesterday

Your friend

R M Bucke

(52)

To Walt Whitman

[London, Ont.,] 24 April [188]9

Your welcome card of 22^d to hand this morning. By same mail a letter from W. J. Gurd—he is getting on well with the gas meter and writes in excellent spirits. All goes well with us here, we are having at the present moment a splendid rain which will do a lot of good. The trees are coming into leaf rapidly /and/ in a few more days at the present rate the country will be green. I have the Tribune you sent me con^g an acct. of the John Hopkins Hospital. Walt, if I were in your fix I would think seriously of going there for the next six months or a year (or even longer, but that would depend) as a private patient. They might do you good (they will have the best skill going) and if they did not you would be more comfortable there than anywhere else perhaps in the world. If you would think well of this I would go to Baltimore— make all the arrangements and then take you from Camden to the Hospital. [—] There is no palace in Europe so comfortable for a sick or half sick man as this hospital would be. Think this over seriously (it is worth it)[.] Show this letter to Horace and talk it over with him (but H. does not half realize as I do the boon such a change would be to you)[1]

Love to you dear Walt

R M Bucke

P. S. I enclose the cutting that you may look it over again if you feel to. The more I think of it the more I think you *decidedly* ought to go—

R M B.

N. B. I do not suppose the expence would be much more than the present subsidy but if it is we can easily get more money

R M B.

---

[1]Neither Whitman nor Traubel showed much enthusiasm for Bucke's plan. Whitman showed Traubel Bucke's letter, and the two of them 'talked over the place and the advisable course somewhat, but in a general, non-personal way that

struck me as peculiar in both of us' (Traubel, V, 85). Traubel also notes that Whitman remarked to Wilkins: 'I should rather eat my crust on my own dung hill than a good meal on another's' (Traubel, V, 92). He sums up his own feelings in the following way: 'As to the hospital, he [Whitman] seems absolutely disinclined. I do not argue against, but there is one point which Bucke does not mention even and which to W. seems the most important of all, viz.—that at the best, W.'s going to Baltimore would involve some sacrifice of freedom' (Traubel, V, 139).

(53)

To Horace Traubel

Asylum, London, Ont. 24 Ap. 89

Have just written W. urging that he go to John Hopkins Hospital to live. See the letter. Let me know how he takes the proposal & what you think of it. Best accts. from Gurd. The meter bus. looks bigger & bigger.

Your friend
R M Bucke

(54)

To Horace Traubel

[London, Ont.,] 4 May [188]9

My dear Horace

I have yours of 2[d]. I had no thought of W. going to Baltimore untill after the book was published. At least if he continued tolerably well. I was only "afraid" (rather, inclined to think) that you would oppose the move just as most folk oppose their friends going to Hospitals and Asylums from a feeling against it. At such a hospital as this (especially with Osler at the head of it—he being really a friend of W's) W. would be infinitely better off than where he is. His surroundings would be unexceptionable and all that modern medicine could do /to/ increase his comfort and improve his condition would be brought into requisition. It is simply monstrous that such a man as W. with friends who are willing to do *any thing* to assist him /and with some means & income of his own/

124

should live as he is doing at present. [—] Poor O'Connor is evidently going down, down, and except for the shock it would give W. I would gladly have him go, for his life must be a burden to him, poor fellow. I am glad to hear that the book is likely to be "on time". [—] That Hartmann affair was bad, very bad.[1] I wrote a note to the Herald for the "Personal Intelligence" Column quoting from a P. C. of W[s] of 17th April as follows: "The sayings of S. H. make H /yourself of course/ (an intimate friend of W.W.[s]) frantic angry—they are invented or distorted, most horribly. I take it all phlegmatically" [/] but it seems the H. did not print it. What do they care who feels bad so the paper sells. But S. H. is the party to blame [/] damn him

RMB

---

[1]C. Sadakichi Hartmann gave a distorted account of some of Whitman's opinions in 'Walt Whitman. Notes of a Conversation with the Good Gray Poet by a German Poet and Traveller', New York *Herald*, 14 April 1889.

(55)

To Walt Whitman

[London, Ont.,] 13 May [188]9

So our dear friend O'Connor is gone at last. Thank God that he died peacefully, without pain. My greatest regret is that with his magnificent abilities he should have done so comparatively little to keep his name alive. However he will be long remembered—if for nothing else—for the "Good Gray Poet" which will not be forgotten for a while yet. His death will be a great grief and also a relief for Mrs O'C. the care of him was always more than she could bear. She will of course grieve bitterly but for her sake I am glad his life was not prolonged if it had been she must have broken down and that would have made things worse than ever. I believe, dear Walt, that it is all right and as it should be—and I trust when I come to die myself, as I must and ought in a little while, that I shall say the same thing. [—] "We shall go to him though he will not come back to us" and when we *do* go to him we shall see that these things are better managed than they would be if we had our way with them. [—] Mrs. O'Reilly (wife of the Inspector of Asylums) died yesterday morning—I go to Toronto to the funeral tomorrow—back next day. [—] So we go one after the other—but it is all right—what good would it be to stay?

Your friend
R M Bucke

(56)

To Walt Whitman

[London, Ont.,] 3 June [188]9

I have today the new L. of G. "31 May 1889." It is a lovely little book. I am thoroughly delighted with it. [—] I have a few cuttings from Eastern papers this evening (sent by a friend) in re dinner. Very glad to see that you were actually present and (more than I expected) spoke a few words. I shall hope to have the papers in full and some short account of the affair in M.S. from you or Horace. I judge from what I see in the papers that the dinner was a success. I am rejoiced, dear friend, that you have stayed with /us/ to get out the *big* and *last* eds. and for this dinner[/] It will surely be patent to all now that you have *come to stay*—patent or not /to the rest/ it is to me an evident fact. It is wonderfull how much more *grip* you seem to have on the world now than even five years ago and the last year even has made an immense difference. Yes, Walt, you are undoubtedly an institution and if I live another twenty years (which is doubtfull!) I shall not be surprised to see my highest claims for you (for making which I have been counted a lunatic[1]) broadly and even generally allowed. My copy of Sarrazin[2] has come to /hand/ by this afternoon's mail—it is as you

126

said, a lovely little book. [—] Our spell of dark, cold, rainy weather has let up at last and we have summer again—not very warm yet but getting warm—it is now 5 P.M. a charming warm, bright evening.— Our lilacs are out and the grounds look well

Love to you, dear Walt
R M Bucke

[1]Richard Watson Gilder, the editor of the *Century Illustrated Monthly Magazine* and the most distinguished guest at the Whitman birthday dinner, referred to Bucke as 'that Canadian crank'. Although Gilder made this remark to Harned in private, Harned repeated it to both Whitman and Traubel. Whitman, of course, defended Bucke: 'Bucke is no crank at all—he is simply individualistic. If to be individualistic is to be a crank, then he is one—not otherwise' (Traubel, V, 265; see also 154–55). Traubel may have passed on Gilder's estimate to Bucke himself, thus prompting this defense.

[2]Gabriel Sarrazin, *La Renaissance de la poésie anglaise, 1798–1889* (Paris, 1889).

(57)

To Walt Whitman

[London, Ont.,] 18 Oct [188]9

I wrote a note this morning and this evening have received yours of 16th enclosing Fanny Grunde's quite affecting little letter and Mrs Spaulding's card. You ask me whether there is any thing I desire Ed. to bring me from Camden. I do not know that there is except the pictures w̄h I mentioned in mine this morning. I mean the little collection of Photo's and engravings which you are about issuing. I suppose you do not want to send that 1872 L. of G.? and I do not want you to send it untill you are quite ready—but do not let somebody else carry it off! [—] I suppose you never found that copy of Harrington?[1] I have never been able to get a copy and it seems as if I never should get one. [—] Yes, I think we may flatter ourselves that L. of G. has got a *locus standi* at last. No one now (unless inspired by ignorance as well as stupidity) can hoot at the book as the *uncu' guid*[2] thought well to do

127

awhile ago. L. of G. has come to stay and must be seriously considered by all serious men henceforth whether they like it or whether they don't—what the outcome of the consideration will be (on the whole) I for one have no fear. I asked you this morning whether you had a man engaged in Ed's place—I hope you will tell me this as I am anxious about it

Love to you

R M Bucke

---

[1]*Harrington: A Study of True Love* (Boston, 1869), was O'Connor's abolitionist novel.
[2]"Unco' guid" is a Scots expression meaning very good or strictly moral people.

(58)

To Horace Traubel

[London, Ont.,] 31 Dec [188]9

My dear Traubel

I have your long and welcome letter of 26[th][.] (Should have answered it a day or two earlier had it been possible, w̄h it was not). [—] I am quite anxious to see Symonds letter which I hope will reach me soon.[1] Shall not forget your request concerning it and whether I send it you or not you shall have the use of it when the time comes. [—] Yes, it is most comforting and most remarkable how well W. has done and how well he is. May he keep so! I for one am not ready to lose him yet! [—] No, I can do nothing in the Danish line. Have tried several Danish friends at Schmidt's old review[2] but have made nothing of it so far—but, all in good time. "All comes to those who know how to wait!" [—] About translating Sarrazin—I have a scheme of my own which I will unfold to you one of these days. If I am able to carry it out I shall publish a translation of S. in a good permanent form along with other matter. I do not believe the pub[n] of S. could be made to pay (in money) in any way but would

128

say nothing to discourage any one. [—] I hope great things from your Whitman paper. Yes, make it personal by all means, and put it in as simple a narrative form as possible. Yes, nothing could be better (as an illustration) than the last Aug. photo.[3] (which looks across the room at me as I write). A photo of the "den" too (if it could be well done) w^d be most interesting (wonderfully so to those who have been in it more or less often). "Walt Whitman at date" would do:[4] how would you like:

"W. W. as I know him"

But (after some hundreds of them) I am a little tired of papers, paragraphs, sonnets &c. &c. &c. called "Walt Whitman" in any shape. [—] How would something like one of the following titles do? (of course I have no pretention to *name* a paper I have not even seen):

"The Poet of the Modern"
"The First American Poet"
"The Avatar of Democracy"
"The Bard of the Dawning Era"

Yes, W. told me about the Lot in the cemetary.[5] That is settled I guess, and satisfactorily as far as I can see.

My mature and settled opinion is that the "Camden Compliment"[6] has been and *is* a great success. I believe it already has done and will do much good and can do (in no case) any harm. I have shown it to parties strange or hostile and notice that they have been much struck with it. It was a good thought, well carried out and all concerned have reason to feel content. [—] I am a little disgusted that you have any (the least) trouble abt. the fund. [—] The money should be sent you not only freely but gladly (as a priviledge) but we must take these things as they come. The main thing is to keep it going. It would never do to have any hitch or hitches interfere with it now. [—] Glad to hear about Chubb and his lecture on a life of W. W. "à la bonne heure"![7] [—] I wonder how many "Lives" of W, *you* will see before you die! [—] For my part I think I shall like to join W. as soon as I can get settled after he is gone

Your friend

R M Bucke

I enclose a P. O. order for 1 Jan '90 payable to T. B. H. as usual

RMB

---

[1]On 25 December 1889, Whitman wrote Bucke: 'J A Symonds from Switzerland has sent the warmest & (I think sh'd be call'd) the most *passionate* testimony letter to L. of G. & me yet—' (WW 2168; for the Symonds letter see Schueller and Peters, III, 424–25).

[2]Rudolf Schmidt's 'Walt Whitman, det amerikanske Demokratis Digter', which appeared in *Ide og Virkelighed* in 1872, was eventually translated by R. M. Bain and Bucke. It is reprinted in part in *In Re Walt Whitman*, pp. 231–48.

[3]Traubel used this photograph, by Gutekunst, as the frontispiece for the fifth volume of his book.

[4]Traubel accepted this suggestion, and 'Walt Whitman at Date' appeared in the *New England Magazine*, 4 (May 1891), 275–92.

[5]The lot in Harleigh Cemetery (see WW 2166 and 2168).

[6]Horace Traubel, ed., *Camden's Compliment to Walt Whitman, May 31, 1889; Notes, Addresses, Letters, Telegrams* (Philadelphia, 1889).

[7]E. W. Chubb published a piece on Whitman in *Stories of Authors* (New York, 1926), pp. 385–92.

(59)

To Walt Whitman

[London, Ont.,] 25 Jan [18]90

I have yours of 22^d. I am glad you are coming round to the Hospital scheme. It is (of all others) *the* scheme for you. You may live for years, you cannot get much (if any) stronger and may get much more helpless. In a good hospital you would be surrounded by absolutely capable attendants (doctors and nurses) and *whatever* happened you would be properly cared for and made as comfortable as skill and science could make you. I know your powers of endurance, they are (like the rest of your faculties) out of the line of ordinary. But what use to tax them unnecessarily? I believe with care and skill properly directed you might even yet have many a good week and month while I fear as at present situated you have mighty few. [—] I will make enquiry about Johns Hopkins (that is a palace of medical skill and physical comfort for the sick and helpless) Baltimore and let you know. If a change is decided on I shall go and see you moved and settled. Don't forget to send me the "poemet".[1] Where is Symonds letter? I should like much to see Steads "Review of Reviews"[2] please send it. [—] I think you are right not to trouble about the money (income) matter.[3] If money is needed it will be found.

We are better here—La Grippe is "letting up" on us and things are beginning to resume their old course

I send my love to you

R. M. Bucke

[1]'Old Age's Ship & Crafty Death's'.
[2]William T. Stead sent Whitman a copy of the *Review of Reviews* (WW 2177).
[3]On 22 January 1890, Whitman wrote Bucke: 'Perhaps I had better tell you, dear Maurice, that the money or income question is the one that *least* bothers me—I have enough to last' (WW 2177).

(60)

To Walt Whitman

[London, Ont.,] 29 Jan [18]90

I have a line from Osler this moment. In answer to mine asking if they would look after you in Johns Hopkins. I enclose the note.[1] I do not understand all of it fully but this much is clear that for about $25. a week (which seems to me we could easily afford) you could be accomodated and provided with *every thing*—of course before taking any step we would find out *every thing* and I would visit Johns Hopkins myself—I will write again tomorrow when I get Osler's further letter promised in this one

R. M. Bucke

[1]This note comes from the Feinberg collection at the Library of Congress:

131

[209 W. Monument Street]

27/1/90

Dear Bucke

Perfectly feasible, I should say. I will talk with Hurd about it. The rates in the private wards run from $25 a week which includes everything. He would be most comfortable & there are so many who would take an interest in him & cheer him up. Will write tomorrow after I see Hurd—

sincerely yours

Wm Osler

P. S. I will reserve one of the best rooms for you.—engage it for 1920 [*sic*] october & part of november

(61)

To Horace Traubel

PRIVATE

[London, Ont.,] 29 Jan [18]90

My dear Horace

You know that for a long time I have thought (and I believe you have thought the same) that Walt Whitman should have more comfortable surroundings and to this end I have from time to time urged him to live in some good hospital where he would be regularly seen by good D^{rs} and waited on and provided suitably. I could never get from W. any consent to this scheme and for a long time I have ceased to urge it—have not mentioned it for months—I was surprized therefore when I got the other day a letter (written 22^d inst.) containing the following passage: "If I had a good hospital well conducted—some good nurse—to retreat to for good I sometimes think it would be best for me—I shall probably get worse & may linger along for some time—of course I know that death has struck me and it is only a matter of time—but may be quite a time yet." [—] Upon receipt of this letter I wrote to W. saying how glad I was that he had taken that notion and how much better off in many ways he would be in a good hospital. At the same time I wrote to Osler of Johns Hopkins asking him whether W. could be received there as a pay patient—what the rate would be &c. [—] I have just received Osler's answer this afternoon saying that there w^d be no difficulty about W's reception and that the pay for every thing would be about $25. a week. This letter of Osler's I have sent to W. Osler is to write me again more in detail *at once*—this letter also no doubt I shall send to W. [—] I should be sorry to have W. out of daily reach of you & Harned but in all other respects the difference between his present life and life at Johns Hopkins would be like the difference between a laborer's life and that of Vanderbilt—the difference would be far more than that because at Johns Hopkins he would get (besides all other good provisions & attendance) the constant, daily, services of the best physicians in America—in the world, perhaps, and this would be of immense importance to him in his present state—I have little doubt that at Johns Hopkins his life would be made greatly more bearable—even comfortable. [—] You see of course why I write you—I want you (as I know you can) to forget yourself—your own feelings—and help me to move W. to this step. [—] Should it be once settled that W. will go I propose to at once visit Johns Hopkins, see just what accommodation he would have—arrange all details and come on to Camden to take W. on to Baltimore—and I should hope that you and perhaps others would go too.[—] About the payment of $25. a week or even more—surely there could be no difficulty (?) W. would perhaps like to pay some part of the rate himself (?) or if not surely you could run the subsidy up to this amount—I would wilingly make my $3. a month $5. others would no doubt do the same or new names could be got? the payment of twice the amount ought not to be any difficulty. [—] Should I go to B. to look into the sort of provision they would make for W. at J. H. perhaps you or Harned would meet me there and look into the matter along with me so that you would be quite satisfied with the step before it was made (?)

Have a talk with Walt on this subject (get him to open it

if possible) and tell me how he feels about it and very fully
what you and Harned think of it.[1]

Willy Gurd has been here all January but has been sick
("La Grippe") all the time. At one time (3 weeks ago) I
feared he would die. He is now slowly recovering—the gas
meter is made—we may establish a Co. to manufacture
here under the Canadian patents to prove the thing practically—we have done nothing yet as Gurd got sick almost
immediately after his arrival here and is so still—I have
good faith in both the gas and water meter

Your friend
R M Bucke

---

[1]In early March the hospital scheme was abandoned. On 6 March Bucke wrote
Traubel: 'I am quite content to let the hospital matter rest for the present and I
think all you say on the subject very reasonable' (Feinberg: LC).

(62)

To Harry Buxton Forman

London, 17 June '90

My dear Harry

A thousand thanks for the Supplimentary Keats Col.
which came to hand this afternoon. The dedicatory verses
to Guen[1] are lovely. Give G. my love and congratulations
on having already a book dedicated to her. It is quite a
distinction for ein junges Fraulein. I have been east and
have seen a good deal of Walt Whitman—from middle of
May to 1st June. 31st May (birthday) we had him to dinner at Preiser's Philadelphia—a "distinguished company"
being present. Col. Robert Ingersol made the most extraordinary extempore speech on record. To me it seemed
supranatural. Such images, such language, such depth of
thought and feeling—it took us all clean off our legs. W.
W. was charmed (not overcome—he is equal to whatever
may happen, good or ill). He thanked Ingersol, shook
hands with him across the table. We all cheered right

lustily—and (as that dear old cynic Carlyle says) "our sublime heads touched the stars". W. is aging—has aged considerably in the last 15 months—doubt if he can see another birthday—but he may for he had a grand constitution under it all.

Had a letter from dear old Jack Harkness today—he has been very ill for six months, dyphtheria (caught from a patient)—gastritis—abscess of the lung and now (he fears) phthisis. I greatly fear Jack is in a bad way. I have written him to come here if he can—as soon as he can.

The meter has not exfoliated into double eagles yet but is incubating and will hatch out yet. All in good time. Love to Guen. Kind regards to all—Affectionately.

R. M. Bucke

I do not ask you to write. No good.

¹Forman's daughter.

(63)

To Horace Traubel

[London, Ont.,] 26 July [18]90

My dear Horace

Yours of 23d to hand yesterday and has been read with much interest. I do not know what I could tell you about Kennedy's visit—we talked a great deal and had a good time and that is abt. all there is to say. *Of course* I said nothing about your notes, it was understood between you and myself that I was not to mention them and I have not and shall not do so—I quite agree with you that the fewer know of them at present the better.¹ I send you herewith ½ a dozen copies of "Sanity"² give one to Dr Brinton yourself please, I am not sure of his address or should have sent him one sooner.

Walt's letters the last month have been unusually bright and cheery—they show absolutely no mental failure. But my opinion (or rather my knowledge of his condition) does not change. I fear a sudden attack which if it comes will probably bring the end in a few hours or days. His brightness does not cheer me because I know how often unusual mental clearness and lightness immediately precedes one of the attacks I allude to. I know he is terribly weak, that there is already damage to important nerve centres—the running gear is worn thin, thin it may go on a long time yet (I have patients now who have been in a similar condition for years and still they live) but it is liable to give way any moment—what saves him (and has saved him) is his *refusal* of emotion—if he would worry, or fret, or get into tempers he would last no time—as it is he has struck an even and an easy gait and he may keep the track a long time—but we must *watch and be ready*. Walt tells me that he has not written the O'C. note[3] but that he certainly will—I feel sure he wants to do it—guess he is waiting for the mood which may be postponed by his weakness which of course has its mental side.

I will keep in mind what you say as to little pieces for "Conservator"—but if you knew how loaded up with work I am! Well, we shall see.

What you say about perhaps *not* coming here this year is far from pleasant reading to me—I had looked upon it as settled and I really want to see you here—do not give up the notion of it—I shall still hope you will see your way—In spite of appearances I am about as poor as yourself—if this meter does not do something for me, the outlook is bad for anything more than a bare living. 5 boys and 2 girls to provide for is no joke let me tell you— you may know it some day yourself! [—] But I still look to the meter to see me through and I still hope to find a way that it may benefit you too. [—] I expect Gurd home almost any day now and we shall steam up the factory as soon as may be after that. [—] We are incorporated (as I guess you know) "The Gurd Meter Co. Limited"—is the style of it. Capital stock $45,000 (U. S. *not* included in

Co's assets). *Par* is offered for stock at present but there is none for sale on those terms. I look to see the stock worth something like a thousand p.c. over par soon after we begin manufacturing

Your friend
R M Bucke

[1]As we see, Bucke and Traubel attempted to keep Traubel's daily record of his visits to Whitman a secret from the other disciples.
[2]This paper was delivered by Bucke at the annual meeting of the Association of Medical Superintendents of American Institutions for the Insane and was published in the *American Journal of Insanity*, 47 (July 1890), 17–26.
[3]The preface to O'Connor's *Three Tales* (Boston, 1892).

(64)

To Walt Whitman

[London, Ont.,] 20 Aug [18]90

I wrote the date as above on 20ᵗʰ and have not had a moment since in which to write the letter

It is now *22 Aug.* and in the first place I may say that I received by mail from England nearly a week ago J. A. Symonds' "Essays: Speculative & Suggestive", that I have, of course, found time to read "Democratic Art", and that I am greatly disappointed.[1] [—] It, to my mind, comes far short of what such a man ought to have written on such a subject. The singular thing to me is that he does not seem to understand the least what you are driving at, what you are *there for*. He speaks for instance of "Walt Whitman whose whole life has been employed in attempting to lay foundations for a new national literature."[2] [—] It is not extraordinary that he should not see through and behind this (perfectly true as far as it goes) phase of the matter? [—] How strange too (to cite a small but significant point) that he does not know that the "Poetry of the Future" is included in "Sp. Days & Collect"?[3]

The whole article is "flat, stale, and unprofitable"—a saw dust chewing business—dealing with the hull, the shell,

the superfices, never for one line, one flash of insight pene-
trating to the heart of the business. Too bad, too bad. I
have your note of 18th, Have not seen the "Rejoinder" you
mention.[4] Will you not send it? Or do you mean the reply
to the Woodberry shirt sleeve lie?[5] I have that & Kennedy's
letter. I hope you will find Symonds' letter & send it, am
particularly anxious to read it now and compare it with his
"Democratic Art" (it *may be* he has purposely kept to the
outside, the form in "D. A."[)] All well here and going
well—only *too much work*

Love always

R M Bucke

[1]John Addington Symonds, *Essays Speculative and Suggestive*, 2 vols. (London, 1890).

[2]Symonds's thesis is that only one contemporary author has addressed himself to 'the cardinal fact of our epoch, to the advent of the people': 'I allude to Walt Whitman, whose whole life has been employed in attempting to lay foundations for a new national literature. Whatever we may think about Whitman's actual performance, it is impossible to neglect his teaching or his practice, when we entertain the question of Democratic Art' (1907 ed., pp. 239–40).

[3]In a letter to Whitman of 3 August 1890, Symonds said that he had discovered this error and hoped to correct it in future editions. According to Schueller and Peters, he never did (see Schueller and Peters, III, 481–82, 484*n*).

[4]Whitman's 'rejoinder' was a discussion of some points raised by Symonds in 'Democratic Art'. It was published as 'An Old Man's Rejoinder' in *The Critic*, 17 (16 August 1890), 85–86, and reprinted in *Good-Bye My Fancy*.

[5]In *Talks with Ralph Waldo Emerson* (1890), Charles J. Woodbury claimed that Emerson had reported seeing Whitman coatless at a dinner party. Whitman refuted the charge in an anonymous 'rejoinder' published in both the Camden *Post* (12 August) and *Lippincott's Monthly Magazine* (March 1891) (see *Corr.*, V, 70*n*– 71*n*).

(65)

To Walt Whitman

22 Sept. '90

Yours of 19th enclosing Wallace's note just received. There
is more "non aurthodox Passion" among your friends than
perhaps you are aware of. Though we do not get up and
curse the (modern) Pharisees as Christ (or far more likely
his friends did) yet we feel it. It is *there* all the same. We do

not and cannot go with Ingersoll in his reprisals and de-
mands but we like the man and we should be foolish to do
any thing to deter him from giving us his friendsh[ip] and
support. We want the conservative orthodox folk (all we
can get of them) and we are getting a good many (I have a
letter this morning from a young presbyterian clergiman—
a good friend of yours) but we want (to my mind) the
independent freethinkers even more since the immediate
future (I fancy) belongs to them. [—] I think you are right
to stand aside (personally) from this I. demonstration but
for my part (as a friend of the cause) I look upon it (and
think you should) with great complacency. I think therefore that you are entirely wrong to be "annoyed" at a demonstration in your favor even if it were entirely by free-
thinker—they cannot alter you or your teaching (on the
contrary) you will undoubtedly, in the end, alter many of
them and will have (in the end) in all probability your most
extreme partisans & lovers [fro]m this section of humanity.
As for I. being ["]solicited" it seems to me that is neither
here nor there—your friends have a right to do what seems
best to them in such matters—their action does not affect
you—you stand aside and let them act. That is all. For my
part nothin[g] w[o]uld give me greater satisfaction than a
rousing demonstration on the part of I. and his friends and
I shall take part in it (if I can) with a good heart. [—] I do
heartily agree with you however in wishing that the affair
could come off in N. Y. Could not this be arranged?[1] I shall
write to Johnston on this point.

All well here, fine weather, Western Fair going on in
London. Meter moving slowly but satisfactorily

Best love to you
R M Bucke

[1]On 19 September 1890, Whitman had written Bucke: '—Ab't the Ingersoll affair I
am in favor of *New York* decidedly, but it is probable they will have it in Phila:—
there is some opposition to me or my cause being identified with I. wh' seems to
make the special I[ngersoll] and freethinking folks more intense in identifying

139

this W W affair with mark'd freethinking and non-orthodox (almost) passion—all of wh' is annoying to me . . . I do not like Col. I being solicited to do this as he appears to have been—' (WW 2301; see also letters 62 and 67).

(66)

To Walt Whitman

London, 22 Nov [18]90

"A mere improvisation"![1] But what is the use, dear friend, of writing poems like this to Harper's or any monthly or for the people who read such publications?

If I know any thing of L. of G. or of you this is one of the most subtle, extraordinary little poems you ever wrote and so far from its being done off-hand it seems to me deeper than the deepest study—even to follow in thought the (double) meaning of it makes me feel giddy as in looking up, up, into the far sky. But what's the use, not 10 people of all who read the piece in Lippencotts will have the remotest idea what it is about—but, along with the rest, by and by, the true readers will come, and you, and the rest /of the Leaves/ being understood, this will be also—that is as far as such fairy—etherial touches, hints, can be understood or comprehended. Am glad to hear that the "belly-ache" is easier—hope it has (or will have) passed off entirely by this time.

All quiet here—pleasant autumn weather—cool, not too cold yet—pleasant driving— [—] All same as ever with meter—i. e. "getting ready to begin" manufacturing—I expect we shall commence turning out meters quite early in the year and I do not know but this is soon enough—all well and all goes well

I send you my love

R M Bucke

[1]On 18 November 1890 Whitman sent Bucke a printed slip of 'To the Sun-Set Breeze', published in *Lippincott's Monthly Magazine* in December 1890. The reference to 'a mere improvisation' is not clear—Whitman does not use the phrase in the letter in which he enclosed the poem. This notation may have been made

on the printed slip. Bucke's interpretation of the poem is discussed in Chapter Five below.

(67)

To Horace Traubel

[London,] 23 Nov [18]90

My dear Horace

I have yours of 20 & 21 inst. Am real glad to hear that you are to revise the "Truthseeker" pamphlet and I do not know but that is after all the best way for the Ingersoll address to come out.[1] It will, in this way, go to the right people—the Ingersoll folk, those who are likeliest to be influenced by it—you know we don't want to call the righteous *only* but *sinners* to repentance! A card fm̄ W. yesterday written 20th he says "the worst of belly-ache over but just a reminder sometimes." I trust there will be no serious return—if there is I should be very anxious. Yes, Bush is a good fellow—I like him much[/] when you see him give him my remembrance & love—tell him I do not & shall not forget him. [—] Glad to hear your W. W. piece progresses—it will give me the greatest gratification to see it and read it in print—be sure you send me a copy *in the journal* the earliest possible moment—then I shall send to my N. Y. bookseller for a supply.— [—] Yes, you must be making some grand notes these days—I can fancy my self an old, old man and you a middle aged one, W. gone from us years ago, living on these notes then printed—reading them and discussing them—never tiring of them—and how many hundreds, thousands, millions after you & I are dead and gone and but for our conversation with W. W. forgotten! I really think, Horace, that you are today doing perhaps the most important work of any man now living.

I am gratified to hear of you and your friends reading "Mans Moral Nature"—I have never gone back on that book—think as well of it as I ever did—and I know that there is a true inspiration at the heart of it.

141

Shall hope to hear early in the week that Mitchell[2] or some other good man has seen W. and trust the opinion formed will be favorable—but, Horace, we are standing on a narrow ledge above a precipice—don't forget it.

Love to you

R M Bucke

---

[1]The address, 'Testimonial to Walt Whitman', was published in *The Truth Seeker,* 17 (November 1890), 690–93, 700.
[2]Dr. J. K. Mitchell, son of Whitman's friend Dr. S. Weir Mitchell.

(68)

To Walt Whitman

22 Dec [18]90

The best letter I have had for a long time was one this moment received written by Dr. Mitchell jr. to Horace and forwarded me by the latter. [—] This letter gives an account of the analysis of your Water and according to it your kidneys are absolutely *sound.* There is nothing at all wrong with your water works except the enlarged prostate and the irritation consequent upon it. Your main difficulty is that on account of the enlargement of the prostate the bladder is not entirely emptied at any time—the urine retained undergoes decomposition and caused irritation—now what is wanted is that a catheter should be passed morning and evening and all the water drawn off (in this way) twice a day. This would have to be done by a doctor for a time but there is no reason whatever that Warren[1] should not learn to do /it/ as well as any doctor after being instructed and provided with a proper catheter. I shall hope to hear that this matter is put upon a proper footing *at once* and after this is done I have every confidence that I shall hear of your being more comfortable than for a long time back.
All well here—glorious weather—but alas! our snow is gone and we have to use wheels again.
All quiet with the meter—too quiet! we do not get on

nearly as fast as I should like but if we go slow I have confidence that we are going sure and now that I am relieved about your kidneys I have good hopes you will be with us to have the "good time coming"

R M Bucke

[1]Warren Fritzinger replaced Edward Wilkins as Whitman's nurse in October 1889.

(69)

To Horace Traubel

22 Dec [18]90

My dear Horace

Many thanks for D[r] Michell's letter which I return—the exam. is *most favorable* showing no disease but the enlarged prostate and its results—i. e. retained urine and irritation of bladder therefrom. I have written W. congratulating him and telling him that his urine should be drawn off with a catheter morning and evening—that a good doctor being got to do this for a time Warren could be taught to do it and that in this simple way his comfort might be materially increased. I wish you could arrange to have this done. My mind is grealy relieved by this letter—of course there remains the paralysis, W[s] age, and his generally enfeebled condition and above all his weak heart so we must not jump to the other extreme and consider him in robust health—nevertheless his kidneys being *sound* as they undoubtedly are is a tremendously important matter and I consider today that W. may be with us for years—although I do not forget that he *may* have died of heart failure before you get this letter. Altogether, however, I feel much better, greatly relieved in fact—I hope some arrangement may be made by which W[s] bladder may be *entirely emptied* morning and evening.

All well & quiet here

Your friend
R M Bucke

(70)

To J. W. Wallace

3 Jan. 18[91]

J. W. Wallace Esquire

Dear friend, I have yours of 13th ult. Have just wrapped up the "Address"[1] and mail it along with this. I think it only right that I should tell you that I have had the "address" type-written and have stored it away among my precious possessions. Of course I sh[d] never make the "address" public unless by arrangement with yourself—nor have I any thought of the kind at present. My hope is that eventually *you* may see your way yourself to publish it in some shape—meanwhile I leave it entirely in your hands as before I saw it at all only I could not let it pass out of my hands in such a way that I might never see it again.

That ordinary men under extraordinary conditions break through (as it were) into the infinite and get a glimpse of what goes on there. That extraordinary men such as Whitman, Isaiah, Paul, John, Swedenborg (?) Blake (?) Jean Paul live a greater or lesser part of their lives in more or less clear view of it is what we must all grant. What I want to know at present is: Is mankind, in its forward march, approaching nearer and nearer the divine land so that one day such a life as Whitman's (for example) will be an ordinary human life?[2] Tell me what you think about this?

I am surprised to hear from you that the members of the "College" did not see the meaning and the importance of the experience you showed them, more especially as they are readers of L. of G. But how blind many apparently good, hearty, honest intelligent readers of W. are to this his main thesis and teaching. You, for instance, are, as far as I know, the first (besides myself) to see the spiritual (the main) meaning of "To the Sunset Breeze."[3]

On Xmas eve I had a fall and dislocated my left shoulder (throwing the head of the humerus into the axilla) I had it at once reduced—have had some little pain and some bad nights since but am, now, I trust, through with the worst

part of it. I am at my office as usual directing the institution with my arm in a sling!
I tell you so that in case you hear about it you will not
fancy I am suffering
I am always

Faithfully yours
R M Bucke

---

[1]Wallace's address of 20 January 1890 to the Bolton disciples (organized in what
they termed 'The Eagle Street College') is cited in Harold Hamer, *A Catalogue of
Works By and Relating to Walt Whitman in the Reference Library Bolton* (Bolton,
1955), p. 50.
[2]This is the thesis of *Cosmic Consciousness*.
[3]Bucke discusses Wallace's experience of 'cosmic consciousness' in *Cosmic Consciousness*, pp. 332–42.

(72)

To Horace Traubel

8 Feb [18]91

My dear Horace

Many thanks for your kind note of 4th and for your kind
and deep interest in my welfare—I feel it more than I can
say—I ought to have sent you & W. word oftener while I
was /sick/ but really it never occurred to me that you would
worry about it—the cheif reason was that I never looked
upon the illness as the least serious and did not have the
sense to think that persons a long way off—knowing less
abt. it might imagine it was so—or at least fear it might be
so. But at all events it is gone by now and I am as well as
usual (which I hope is well enough to satisfy any one). If
you can make the (soi-disant) liberals (or even a few of
them) understand that L. of G. contains the vital religious
fire of today well and good—you will have done a good
work—and at least it is worth trying—good luck to you in
the enterprise! [—] But really it sometimes looks to me (of
late years) as if all this was useless—that those who have it
in them to see—see any how—and that those who have not

will not see or hear "even tho' one rose from the dead to tell them"—but this no doubt is an exaggeration the other way—it is well for us to work anyway for our own sakes if not for the sake of others—therefore work my dear boy "while it is still day—for the night & &"

Yes, Horace, I know I am too much of a savage for the N. Y. folk (and for many others)—but after all who and what is the "friendly and flowing savage?"[1] is he behind or ahead of our boasted civilization? [—] Some time ago I said: "From this moment I ordain myself loosed from all limits."[2] [—] And I find it a very good way to live—let each one do as it suits him. [—] "I am for those who are not mastered—whose tempers cannot be mastered—whom laws, theories, conventions can not master."[3] I am for living the new life *and getting the good of it*—do you know what that means? I am not worrying abt. what folk think or say

Love to you dear Horace
R M Bucke

[1]'Song of Myself', l. 976.
[2]'Song of the Open Road', l. 53.
[3]'By Blue Ontario's Shore', ll. 288–90.

(71)

To Horace Traubel

14 Feb [18]91

Dear Horace

I have two letters from you both dated 10th tho' I think one was written 11th and also I have "The Voice" 15 Jan. with the ethical-culture piece. Thanks very much for it. One of your letters contained the finished "Dutch Traits"[1] which I cannot help thinking one of the most suggestive pieces yet written about our friend. [—] I thank you, my dear friend, for your interest in me on the occasion of my slight illness which would seem much more serious than it really was to your thoughtfull eyes looking at it from 500 ms away. I am thankfull on many accounts (on those you mention not the least so) that my constitution seems perfectly sound and that my prospects of life and vigor seem excellent for a man of my age. That you and I shall need both health & vigor to carry through the work that lies before us during the next few years I well believe and if they are given us we cannot be too thankfull—when all is over and done I believe I shall be ready & willing at any moment to join our friend in the great Hereafter. [—] About the book of pieces on *Walt*— Sarrazin &c I am clearly of your mind and think it should be kept entirely distinct from W's own vol. What should go into it is a grave point—I should say: let us put in (as far as possible) the best things that are not now accessible to the English reader—1—Sarrazin of course—2—I am not so sure about the Ingersoll piece as that is now in fair shape already—3—I think we should have a translation of Knortz piece (do you know it?)—4—of course I would like to have my piece in and would overhaul it carefully—5—If we could have (at least a part of) Rudolph Schmidts piece—Danish—it would be well. 6—Then Kennedy's Dutch Piece—7—Rollestons German piece should be seriously considered &c— &c—Of course all the pieces would need carefull editing— each (at present) has a biographical section which would have to come out and so on—What, too, would you think of Ann Gilchrists piece from the old Radical?[2] Now-a-days few, I fancy, ever see it and it is fine. [—] If this book is got up I will invest $25, in copies of it and perhaps we could sell many copies by subscription.—9—Of course your N. E. Mag. piece would go in.

I have very little to report here—no meters yet! You will think they are never coming—but they are! We shall I think have the first batch in the course of next week. All will yet be right—a little patience, that is all that is wanted

Best and kindest wishes and regards to you
R M Bucke

---

[1]William Sloane Kennedy, 'Dutch Traits of Walt Whitman', *The Conservator*, 1 (February 1891), 90–91.
[2]Anne Gilchrist, 'An Englishwoman's Estimate of Walt Whitman', Boston *Radical*.

(73)

To Walt Whitman

31 March [18]91

re "Goodbye my Fancy"[1]

Ruskin says of great writers that they "express themselves
in a *hidden way* and in parables". I have understood this of
you, Walt, for many a year and I am bold enough to say
that I believe I have followed the subtle winding & bur-
rowing of your thought as far as any one. [—] I have
known well from the first that "there are divine things well
envelop'd—more beautifull than words can tell." It is this
mystic thread—running through all your poems that has
facinated me from the first more than any thing else about
them. I have noted the (by most people) "unsuspected author."—"spiritual, godly, most of all known to my sense."
and I understand (tho' you will never tell—perhaps could
not tell us) where the secret prompting comes from. [—]
Well, the "haughty song—begun in ripened youth—never
even for one brief hour abandon'd." is finished, and the
singer soon departs—and the present listeners soon depart.
But the song remains and will do its work—that same song
is the most virile, potent and live thing on this earth
today—and the singer and listeners they go the way provided for them but they will not get out of the range of this
prophetic utterance. I congratulate you, dear Walt, today
upon having completed the greatest, most divine, most hu-
manly helpfull work that has ever so far proceeded from
any individual man—and this claim for L. of G. I will
maintain while I live

I am, dear Walt

With love and admiration
Your friend
R M Bucke

[1]This letter quotes 'Song of the Open Road' (l. 119), 'Shakspere-Bacon's Cipher' (l.
3), 'To the Sun-Set Breeze' (l. 13), and 'L. of G.'s Purport' (ll. 3–8), all poems from
Good-Bye My Fancy.

(74)

To Horace Traubel

7 May [18]91

My dear Horace

I am *here,* over at office, in good time—a little *lame* yet[1] but otherwise O. K. The New England Magazine reached me from my New York bookseller this A. M. and I need not say the piece[2] has been read. [—] I would like to compliment you upon it but really do not know how to put it—the article is unique and take it all in all I am not sure it is not the best thing yet. We cannot compare it to O.C.'s "Good Gray Poet", to Sarrazin's piece, or Knortz' or Rolleston's—they all have their merits but also the one failing that, viz, they are "literary" while this thing of yours is no picture, disquisition, argument, exposition or reproduction in poetry or prose but is *the thing itself*—W. actually lives in your pages—you can see him and hear him speak. There is not a false note from beginning to end every word *genuine* and just what it should be, neither more nor less. Its only fault is that it ends too soon—I should like a big vol. of just such pages—I could read in it day and night. And by & by (thanks to you) we shall have such vols![3] Think how people today delight to read great volumes of Pepys and Boswell—that being so how much more will they rejoice in years to come to read similar volumes (as characteristic and as truthfull) about this far greater man? My dear boy you are in a great position, you have a big morgage on the future and don't you forget it! [—] I have not heard from either you or W. for two days [/] I trust all is going well

My love to you & heartiest congratulations

R M Bucke

[1]In early April Bucke's foot became inflamed, and he suffered from this condition for several months.

[2]'Walt Whitman at Date'.

[3]He is, of course, referring to the collection eventually published as *With Walt Whitman in Camden.*

(75)

To Walt Whitman

30 June [18]91

Your welcome note of 28th reached me here this a.m. I have not yet received the proof birthday piece which you mention but am well pleased to learn that it has been sent & shall look anxiously each mail for it (perhaps it will be here before this afternoon). No hitch so far about my getting off by the Britannic on 8th. Expect to leave here Sunday so as to have 30 hours in N. Y. [—] Shall see Johnston if possible. I told you (day or two ago) that I had the note to Tennyson[1]—many thanks! I am glad to hear you are no worse. Keep so at least till I get back to see you! I want to tell you all the English news

Love
R M Bucke

---

[1]The transcript of Whitman's note, from the Weldon collection, reads:

Camden N. J. U. S. America / June 26 '91

> If you are feeling well enough and in opportune mood let me introduce my good friend & physician Dr Bucke—He is Superintendent (medical and other) of the big Insane Canadian Asylum at London Ontario—is an Englishman born but raised (as we say it) in America. I still stick out here in the land of the living but pretty tough pulling most of the time—
>
> Walt Whitman

(76)

To Walt Whitman

[R. M. S. "BRITANNIC."]
7 a. m. Wednesday
8th July [1891]

We are off, dear Walt, in a few minutes. I was glad to see Warry yesterday[1]—Many thanks for the L. of G. tho' of course I had a copy with me, would not think of going so far without one. I have this moment received a cablegram from Johnston & Wallace of Bolton to say that they will write to me *Queenstown*—they are wonderfull fellows, I shall enjoy seeing them immensely

Love to you always
R M Bucke

[1]On 7 July 1891 Warren Fritzinger came to New York to give Bucke Whitman's stuffed canary for presentation to the Bolton disciples (WW 2586 and 2588). Bucke duly brought the bird and an autograph copy of 'My Canary Bird', which it had inspired, to Bolton (Johnston and Wallace, pp. 60*n*—61*n*).

(77)

To Walt Whitman

Bolton, Lancashire
18 July '91

I am really at a loss how to begin this letter or how to write it. My reception here has been such that I am absolutely dumbfounded. I got here about noon yesterday (I ought to say that I had a telegram at Queen's town from Johnston to say that Wallace & he would meet me at L.pool if I w^d let them know the time of my arrival, but I did not think it well to give them that trouble & came through alone)—Johnston & Wallace met me at the station. It was a fine day and I went round the town with Dr J. while he made his daily visits. Sat in the carriage while he went in the houses. [—] We went to a hotel to dinner—then 8 of us went for a 20 mile drive through as picturesque a country as I have seen any where—had tea 8 miles from here with another Whitman friend (Rev. Thompson) then he came to Bolton with us. [—] By this time it was after 8 o'clock and on reaching Johnston's house we found a half a room full of men waiting for us—from then to midnight was constant talk, soup, recitations, supper, and good fellowship generally. You are right to say that the Bolton friends are true and tender—they are that and if there are any stronger words you may use them! Most of the evening I laughed and the rest of it I could have cried their warmhearted friendship for you and for me was so manifest and so

151

touching. I enclose a song[1] which they had composed & set to music and which the whole room sang together in the middle of the evening—of course I made a speech of thanks and two other quite long speeches in the course of the evening—and I really spoke quite decently! a wonderfull thing for me. [—] You will of course, dear Walt, show this letter to Horace as there is no use my writing it over again to him. [—] I trust you are no worse than usual—and that I shall find you to the fore when I return in September.

Nothing to tell about the meter yet.

Wallace slept here last night, he and Johnston desired me to say that they might not have time to write you today and wished me to give you their love and assure you of their devotion to you and *the cause*—and indeed, Walt, it looks as if the thing had come here *to stay*—I was to say, too, to you & Warry that the canary had come safe—not even the glass cracked! and that it was warmly appreciated. And I want you to tell Mrs Davis that they all know her here and feel very friendly towards her.

I think I have said all I can at the present moment—will soon write again.

I send you my love, dear Walt, and sign myself yours till death.

R M Bucke

P. S. I read the message from you to the boys here (in your letter of early July[2]) yesterday evening—the boys were much affected by it—they have taken the letter from me to fac simile that part of it so that they may each have a copy

R M B

If it were even possible for you to come to England the fellows would go clean crazy about you.

---

[1]The text, taken from the Weldon collection, is to be sung to 'The March of the Men of Harlech', a Welsh national air:

The College Welcome to Dr Bucke

17 July 1891

Comrade-stranger, glad we greet you.
One and all are pleased to meet you,

Cordial friendship here shall heat you,
   Whilst with us you stay.
Friend of Walt! Be that the token,
That enough our hears to open,
Though no other word be spoken
     Friends are we alway.
   Friendship let us treasure,
   Love to greatest measure,
  Comrades true our journey through:
   Life's thus made a pleasure.
Hail! to Whitman, lover's poet!
Here his portrait. All well know it
To the world we gladly shew it
    Proud his friends to be.
Doctor Bucke, Walt's brave defender,
Thanks to you we gladly tender
Noble service did you render
    To our hero's fame.
You, his chosen "explicator,"
"Leaves of Grass's" indicator,
You, his life's great vindicator
    Honoured be your name
   Health to Walt and glory!
   Long live the poet hoary!
  Noble life through peace and strife
   Immortal be his story!
Let us cherish his example,
Kind, heroic, broad and ample,
Be our lives of his a sample,
    Worthy friends prove we.

W. Dixon

[2]In that letter Whitman wrote: 'Best regards & remembrances to friends all, men and women, the other side— . . . —of course to the dear Bolton friends—(hope the Canary bird box will get there safe) & many & many a one unspecified—I appreciate them all & send best love & thanks (as f'm a flickering well-burnt candle, soon to be all out)—' (WW 2586).

(78)

To Horace Traubel

Bolton, Lancashire
18 July '91

My dear Horace

All here, Johnston & Wallace especially, send loving greetings to you—and Johnston says: "Say to Traubel that the photographs came safely to hand."
I have written Walt giving account of my reception here; you will see that letter and I need not repeat. I may say

however that if nothing comes of my trip but what has already come of it *here* I shall consider the journey a success. We had many little speeches and much talk and I was very greatly gratified to find that they realize the magnitude of this Whitman business just as fully as we do—nothing that I said of the meaning and probable future of Whitmanism (and I spoke out pretty plainly) staggered them at all—they had thought it all before; and I tell you, Horace, I am more than ever (if that is possible) convinced that we are right at the centre of the largest thing of these late centuries. It is a great privilege and will be ages from now a great glory to us. For my part when I stop and think of it I am fairly dazed—the strangest thing, to me, about it all is that I have had premonitions of this spiritual upheaval and of my (small) part in it since I was eight or ten years old[1]—and now it has come—a solid fact and come to stay—and we will stay with it

Love to Anne
and love to you
R M Bucke

The boys here are afraid you are working too hard—pray be carefull of yourself and be sure to take a good rest (not less than 8 hours) every night—do not work so late as to prevent this.

[1]See *Cosmic Consciousness*, p. 8.

(79)

To Walt Whitman

46 Marlborough Hill
St Johns Wood
London N. W.
England
23 July 91

I am staying here with H. Buxton Forman. Have been here 3 days now and shall remain untill about this day week. Go then to make a little visit with Alfred Withers who is also a very good friend of yours but not as crazy about you as some of us are! [—] I have spent this whole day in the house—there was nothing especial to do outside so I worked at the lecture which I have to give in Montreal (to the students there) abt. 1 Oct. I have got the lecture now pretty well under way—I saw Mrs Costelloe day before yesterday for a few minutes on the street—I was going to call on her and met her—the same day I saw Mr. Costelloe for an hour on meter business. I am to see him and some other parties tomorrow about the meter. I hope to see Mr & Mrs Smith in the course of a week or two and to call on Tennyson from there. I am to go to Mrs Costelloes to dinner tomorrow evening and expect to meet Miss Alys there. I saw a letter from Mr Smith to a friend the other day in which he spoke quite warmly of you so I guess if he does not write it is only from want of time—or perhaps his sight is too bad to write much.[1] Any way I will let you know about it later. I am enjoying my visit here and am feeling first class—but I shall not [*sic*] be glad to get back to America & Canada /again/ when the time comes. I would rather be closer to you and other dear friends. Best love to you dear Walt from your friend

R M Bucke

P. S.

Your card of 14th is this moment to hand [/] am well pleased that you seem to keep about the same—no worse I judge any how—Give my love to Horace—will write him soon but I tell you I am pretty busy!

R M B

---

[1]Robert Pearsall Smith and his family had all been close friends of Whitman in Philadelphia, and Whitman was concerned about their attitude toward him. On 6 July he wrote Bucke: 'Best regards & remembrances to friends all, men

and women, the other side—to the Smiths, R. P., Mary, Alys & Logan—
haven't got word f'm them in four months—(have they dropt me?)—' (WW
2586). In three subsequent letters to Bucke, Whitman again sent greetings to
the Smiths.

(80)

To Walt Whitman

46 Marlborough Hill
St Johns Wood
London N. W.
26 July '91

I am so much occupied with the meter and a lot of other
things including work on our W. W. book that I can not
write as often as I sh^d like—but you will be far away wrong
if you think there is any other reason for my comparative
silence. But something has gone wrong with the Smiths and
I may as well tell you first as last. Neither they nor /the/
Costelloes have asked me to visit them and when I dined at
the Costelloes on friday and gave Mrs C. your message to
her and the Smiths she never answered me and never asked
a question about you. But do not let all this worry you, dear
Walt,—there are a few of us left and we will be a legion
when the right time comes.[1] [—] *My* only feeling on the
matter is one of intense curiosity. *Why sh^d* they shift about
in this weather-cock fashion? At Bolton I saw a letter from
Mr Smith to Johnston thanking Johnston for his "notes"[2]
and in that letter he expressed himself as being very much
your friend. Why should he write to J. that way if he had
ceased to be your friend? J. is a stranger to Mr S. & he had no
temptation as far as I can see to pretend any thing to him. I
had some talk with H. B. Forman (I am writing from his
home) on the subject (F. is your friend through & through)
& he thinks that *Mrs S.* & *Mr* Costelloe are responsible for
the coolness[3]—be this as it may the coolness itself is a solid
fact. [—] I have not so far accomplished any thing in meter
matters but the parties who are looking into it seem much

156

interested—I may do something yet before I leave England or I may pave the way for future business. Give my love to Horace and say to him that I will write soon.—My trip is agreeing with me and I am as well and hearty as possible

Best love to you

R M Bucke

[1]Whitman acknowledged receiving this information on 6 August 1891, but did not elaborate: 'Yrs of 26th July this mn'g—(this is the 3d)—Rather blue with me this week—' (WW 2609). He wrote no further letters to the Smiths or the Costelloes, and with the exception of Logan Pearsall Smith, who wrote him twice, received none from them. Logan Pearsall Smith has an affectionate chapter on Whitman in his autobiography, *Unforgotten Years* (Boston, 1939).

[2]Dr. John Johnston, *Notes of a Visit to Walt Whitman* (Bolton, 1890) (privately printed).

[3]Religion may have been at the root of this 'coolness'. Benjamin Costelloe was a staunch Catholic, and Hannah Whitall Smith was a prominent Quaker (see Parker, pp. 3–36, 54–65).

(81)

To Horace Traubel

31 July '91

Kingsgate:

Cricklewood, N. W.

London

My dear Horace

Your good, long and most interesting letter of 20th reached me last evening and has been read and "inwardly digested." A card of 21st from W. came by same mail and it is (as you may well believe) a great comfort to me to hear and know that W. is getting on so well. Was much pleased, too, to hear from you that Mrs. O'C. would go west with me [/] I have quite set my heart on having her make us this visit and shall be greatly disappointed if any thing comes in the way of it. It seems only too certain that the Smiths (including Mrs C.) have gone clean back on W. I do not know that you will approve of the plain way in which I told W. about it (no doubt you will see the letter) but I always think it best to come right out with these miserable businesses and after a clear understanding all round to start fresh on the new basis. I have not time to write you half such a good letter as you in your kindness have written me but you will not think for that that I love you the less. I am as busy as a nailer, spent yesterday afternoon at the British Museum working at the Danish translation & shall work at it this afternoon again. Then the two German have to be done—the *french* will probably have to wait for the shipboard time (L'pool to N.Y.).[1] Meter matters take a lot of my time and all looks well in that direction tho' I doubt much whether I shall accomplish any thing very definite during my present stay here. I am told that Tennyson is much broken in health and mind and sees nobody but I shall attempt to see him & should I succeed shall make as full a note as possible of what transpires. I am very sorry about Clifford[2]—if the meter would only get a move on and assume such proportions as I anticipate (perhaps foolishly) possibly an opening might be found in that direction (?.) Love to W. to Anne and yourself—Write to *old address*—I hope to sail 26 Aug. & see you 2 or 3 Sept.

R. M. Bucke

[1]Translations for *In Re*.
[2]See note to letter 29.

(82)

To J. W. Wallace

Kingsgate
Cricklewood, N. W.
London
[July 31, 1891]

Dear Mr. Wallace,

Many thanks for yours of 29th, enclosing copy of Walt's of 19th.

I send you one just received from Traubel. I do not consider Walt's negative of any consequence, if otherwise you could make up your mind to go.[1] America is large and (as Horace would say) has a large welcome for you in Camden—London, Ont. &c. and I know whatever we might think or say, that Walt would give you as warm a welcome as any of us if you were once across—it is his way to hold off and let people *insist* on seeing and knowing him and if they dont want him bad enough for that—all right. I understand the old man *right through,* he can't hide anything from me and I know he would be immensely pleased and flattered should you go and see him and *all the more so* because you went almost against his express opinion of what was best. W. claims to be "maternal as well as paternal" and he actually does included the feminine nature in his extraordinary personality.

Expect me in Bolton to spend a couple of days with you (as arranged) somewhere from 19th to 24th. (Definite date later.)

Best regards to all the "College".

R. M. Bucke

the above is my address for 10 days
I want Horace's letter back. Keep it for me. R. M. B.

---

[1]Bucke had urged Wallace to return with him to the United States (Johnston and Wallace, pp. 24–25). Wallace then wrote Whitman concerning the proposed visit. On 19 July 1891 Whitman replied:, '—thank the dear friends for urging you to come on a trip to America largely on my acc't, & thank you for considering it but I feel y'r decision in negative is the best and wisest & approve it decidedly— Suppose you have had some tremendous talks with Dr Bucke (he carries heavy guns)—' (WW 2598).

(83)

To Walt Whitman

4 Aug. 91

London, Eng.

Sunday (day before yesterday) I went with Mrs Costelloe from London to Hazelmere. I am confident they had not intended asking me but for some reason they did. Mrs. C. was very nice indeed and I like her as much as ever, neither do I believe that she has altered towards you *really*, but for some reason she is silent on the subject—she did not speak of you at all though we were much together and spoke of every thing else—I avoided the subject waiting to see if she would begin upon it. Once she asked me what I was doing in the British Museum—I said "working at some translation[.]" She wanted to know what translation. I told her something from the Danish for a book some of us were about to bring out.[1] "Well what was the book about?" I said "About Walt Whitman[.]" She said "Oh" and did not pursue the subject. I spent yesterday morning with Mr Smith— he did not speak of you except a very few words, I gave him your message—he scarcely seemed to hear it. Still I believe he is friendly to you in his heart. Mrs S. is *not friendly* [/] she is the only one who said any thing actually unfriendly—she did not say *much* but it was significant. I did not call on Tennyson as it was too late when I got to Hazelmere & too early when I left the next day but I am to spend Saturday afternoon and Sunday there and Mr Smith will take me to Tennyson's. I do not however expect to see T.[2] [—] All goes well, I am hearty and having a good time but shall be glad to get back and see my American & Canadian friends again

Love to you always

R M Bucke

[1]He refers to Schmidt's piece (see letters 58, 71), which he was translating with the help of R. M. Bain.

[2]Bucke went into further details in a conversation with Traubel on 7 September 1891. Traubel's transcript follows (Weldon):

> B. . . . After I had got to England & seen friends there, everybody seemed interested in dissuading me from attempting to see Lord Tennyson. They told me that he was in poor health—especially mentally. In fact, they went so far as to say that he had a nurse—that he was not to be trusted in his movements—that it would have been unsafe for him to go about alone.
> T. And you hesitated?
> B. I confess that I did, at first. They went [on] to make the objections very direct. They told me that he never saw anybody—yes, /they/ even

argued that Walt had no right to send anyone to see Tennyson with a letter.

He was exceeding his privileges. It was pretty certain Tennyson would not see me. And so on, & so on. However, I persisted. I could only reply that I had the letter—

T. And would see whether it would pass current?

B. Exactly—deliver it in any case. If he would receive me, well & good. I would do my part.

T. Walt would have thought it unfortunate if you had yielded to the - clamor.

B. I felt that myself. I wished to leave it with Tennyson to say whether Walt's name was sufficient to open the door for me.

(84)

To Walt Whitman[1]

London W. England / *Monday*
10 Aug '91

On Saturday I went again to the Smith's at Hazelmere. Mrs C. was (and is) away on the continent (Mr C. too). I had plenty of talk with Mr, Mrs, and Alys & Logan S. Logan desired me to send his love to you *he* is very friendly to you, Mr S. only moderately so & Mrs & A. S. *not at all* as far as I can find out. Mrs C. I believe is in her heart friendly but "for reasons" she says nothing—this matter is too delicate to *write* about even to you but I will tell you all when we meet abt. 2^d or 3 Sept. When I returned to town today I found your letters & cards of 24th, 26th & 29th and a couple of letters from H. besides letters from home &c. I am well pleased to see that you keep, if not fairly, at least not markedly worse and I hope to find you "right side up with care" on my return about 2^d Spt. (Not a very long time now). I have the "Lip."[2] and find that the "Dinner Piece" comes out *well*—I think it as good an ad. as we have had. But the main thing I want to talk to you about today is my visit yesterday to Lord Tennyson. I was (as I have said) at Mr S.'s and he sent me with a man & buggy to L. T.'s place some 5 ms. away. I drove thro' one of the wildest and most beautifull pieces of country (in a drizzling rain) that I have seen any where, hills, woods, brush, every-where but with

splendid *English* roads to drive on. Got to T.ˢ (a fine almost
stately mansion) a little before 4 P. M.[,] got out, rang the
bell—a footman opened the door, I gave him your letter
and my card & said "please give these to Lord Tennyson."
He left me in the hall and disappeared in the house—soon
he came back and conducted me into a room on the ground
floor to the left of the main hall—I went in and sat down—
in a few minutes a quite young looking and handsome
man came in—he held out his hand to me and said "good
day Dʳ B." I shook hands with him saying at [the] same
time "you are Hallam Tennyson?" He said he was and we
had a little talk—then after saying that "his father" was
sleeping—that he always lay down for a couple of hours in
the afternoon & would not be up untill 5 o'c. he asked me
if I would wait—I said certainly I would wait if he thought
L. T. would see me. He said "I don't know, but I would
like you to wait" then he asked me if I would step in and
see Lady T. I said I shd be very happy to do so. He took me
to the next room where L. T. was lying on a sofa—a very
pale & delicate but a very spiritual, intellectual & pleasing
face. I sat down by her sofa and we talk[ed] for a good half
hour about Canada & the Canadians—about the late Sir
John Macdonald[,] about Carlyle & Mrs C. (she said they
were not understood, that Froude's book did them injus-
tice—that they were greatly attached to one another &c. [/]
she said she had seen Mrs C. once when some disparaging
remark was made about C. burst into tears) and other
things—then Hallam asked me to go with him up stairs to
see Mrs Tennyson—I went (of course)—Mrs T. is a very
young looking and almost beautifull woman with an air of
considerable distinction—she received me in a half stately
but very kind manner and we had quite a little talk. (I had
been at least half an hour with Lady T. and it was now
nearly 5 o'c. A little before 5 Hallam asked me to go with
him to Lord T.s room—I did so. I found L. T. in a large
room on the first floor (up one stair, as yours is) containing
book shelves and many books—he was sitting on a sofa

and as I went in did not see me so as to know who was there—in fact when I went up to him he thought I was Hallam—I spoke to him and took his hand (which he thought strange thinking I was H. however he soon realized who it was and then welcomed me. We then talked with perfect unconstraint for an hour. T. is not much for compliments, very blunt and down-right—he spoke of you with much good feeling but my reception at the house, by the whole family, was a far greater compliment to you than a volume of soft phrases would have been. [—] None of the Tennyson's I imagine (I had hardly any talk about L. of G. except with Hallam who spoke very freely and pleasantly on the subject) have you read so as really to understand you or what you are after—but have read you enough to know in a more or less vague way that you are a great force in this modern world. Had I been introduced to the Tennysons by the greatest prince in Europe they could not have received me more courteously, nor had I been a near relative could they have shown me greater friendliness—all this of course was for your sake since they did not know of me by name even. But after all I fear I can give you but a faint notion of the pleasure my visit was to me. [—] The Smiths had said that T. was old and queer and that he certainly would not see me—that *perhaps* H. would see me &c. &c. &c. So that I was totally unprepared for the reception they gave me. And the Smith's seemed as much surprised as myself when I went back and told them about it. [—] T.ˢ presence is imposing but does not make as strong an impression of *great personality* as I expected. He is still handsome but so shortsighted that his eyes have little expression. He is not nearly so reserved, carefull and dignified in conversation as I looked for—says (With somewhat rapid enunciation) whatever comes uppermost—said (for instance) "there—I have caught you in an americanism" and then pointed out the phrase. Said "I *hate* that word 'awfully' they might as well say 'bloody' at once—they both *mean* the same". Then showing a lot of pictures

& busts of self and family (different members) done by Ward—Millais &c. &c. he said: "The best of it is they never cost me a penny—they were all done for nothing." [—] I am asked to go back to Smith's but probably shall not as time is getting short. I sail 26th inst. & must leave London for the north about 20 or 21, Mr Costelloe is to be back in town tomorrow and then we see what is to be done about the meter. I have the Danish W. W. piece translated—am now at Knortz' have a lot of work to do yet—give Horace my love and show him this letter—tell him to *keep it*. I may want to see it again as I have no other record of the T. interview—tell him *it must not get out* on any account that would *never do.*

Best love to you dear Walt

R M Bucke

<hr>

[1]Note by Whitman in upper left-hand corner of envelope, 'visit to Tennyson'.
[2]*Lippincott's Monthly Magazine.*

(85)

To Horace Traubel

London W.

11 Aug. '91

My dear Horace

I have your two letters of 27th & 28th very glad to hear such good (not really good but good to what they might be) accounts of Walt. Trust all may be well now till I get back— shall see you, I hope, about 3d Sept. [—] I have told W to give you my Tennyson letter & you will *keep it* I want to see it again myself (perhaps have a copy of it)—I half expected to find a personality in T. in some sense comparable (though far inferior) to Ws. but nothing of the kind. He is not a seer, not a prophet at all but a polished, able, intellectual, high class man [/] *very* high class, in intellect, feeling, candor, high heartedness, purity &c. &c. but not transcendent—nothing of the *God* as in our poet. not a "Beginner" as in the dear old man. [—] Simply the highest and best kind of a singer, the noblest kind of a mere man the divine in whom is as usual buried not shining through evident and unmistakable. But do not fancy that I do not consider T. a great man—he is a great man, a splendid man but he is not a poet in the sense in which *we* have learned to use that word. [—] The hospitality with which I was received not only by T. but by Lady T. Hallam & Mrs T. amazed me and touched me deeply—as I left the house Hallam told me that whenever I came back to England they would all be glad to see me again. [—] This letter and that to W. *must not get out*—it would never do— [—] I am working hard at the translations and hope to have all ready to hand to you when I reach Camden. I hope to get to work at the meter again in a couple of days and a week from now (when I write again) I may have something to tell. [—] I should like to write oftener and more to W & you but my time is very full and it is hard to get even half an hour to scribble in. love to Anne,

Your friend
R M Bucke

(86)

To Walt Whitman

London W.
16 Aug. '91

Yesterday came to my hands your card of 2ᵈ inst. I have not written you as often /as/ I should have liked. Life is at high-pressure here especially when your time is so short as mine on this visit. [—] I have the "Post" with "Over-Sea Greeting" and also the same thing on a slip from Bolton (one of several, I infer, that Horace sent over to Johnston or Wallace). Horace is mighty 'cute to utilize the scraps as he does—it is well, all well, can do no harm and may help.[1] We *must* keep moving, cannot stand still in fact—time for *that* is gone. [—] I expect to spend next Sunday with Carpenter in Milthorpe. then go Monday to Bolton & stay there till wednesday morning—run to L'pool after breakfast and get aboard "Majestic" before noon.[—] She sails abt. noon. [—] I ought to reach N. Y. 1ˢᵗ or 2ᵈ & see you 2ᵈ or 3ᵈ—4ᵗʰ, I think, at latest. Shall be very glad to see you again. I enjoy it over here but "there is no place like home." [—] My visit here has been a great success—I have been well received and treated on all hands, I shall feel richer for it for the rest of my life.

Keep good heart, dear Walt, till I get back—but in any case be easy about "L. of G." and the good cause—*they are all right*

Your loving friend
R M Bucke

[1]Traubel wrote two articles for the Camden *Post* based on the news from Bucke and the disciples at Bolton: 'Over-Sea Greeting; Walt Whitman's Fame Abroad' (1 August 1891) and 'Walt Whitman Abroad' (7 August 1891).

5

'The Christ is dead! Again we have buried the Christ!'

Bucke's most ambitious project during the 1890s was an examination of the human faculty he called 'cosmic consciousness'. Although the term only comes into prominence in this period, the ideas it describes are largely based on the psychological phenomena he first explored in *Man's Moral Nature*, where he sketched the structure of the moral nature, composed of the negative faculties of hate and fear and the positive ones of love and faith. In the concluding chapter of that book he expressed his belief that through the process of evolution the positive faculties were growing in scope and

167

intensity and the negative ones were declining. In the new book, *Cosmic Consciousness,* he now examined fourteen extraordinary and thirty-six ordinary instances of this new faculty.

On 18 May 1894 Bucke spoke on 'cosmic consciousness' in Philadelphia before the American Medico-Psychological Association, and the lecture was published in the proceedings of the association and also as a pamphlet. He completed the manuscript of the book four years later but had difficulties in finding a publisher, in part, he believed, because of the upset caused by the Spanish-American War. In a letter to H. B. Forman of 5 August he commented:

> The whole book trade of the States is suspended until the war is ended—which it will be I trust almost immediately—in fact there can hardly be any more fighting—when the war is ended and business resumed I am in hopes my book will be published and you will have a chance to see just how crazy (?) it is. I am well aware that the book is not based on learning—in fact I shall probably be held up by the smart journals as a first class ignoramus—nevertheless I hope to tell some things not heretofore realized and which are worth knowing.[1]

Man's Moral Nature concluded with Bucke's assurance that 'everything is really good and beautiful, and . . . an all-powerful and infinitely beneficent providence holds us safe through life and death in its keeping forever . . . ' (p. 191). This claim rested on no more than an emotional conviction; but in the opening section of *Cosmic Consciousness* he outlines in specific terms his reasons for this belief. We are on the brink of three revolutions, he says, which will radically and permanently alter human existence—aerial navigation, socialism, and cosmic consciousness:

> Before aerial navigation national boundaries, tariffs, and perhaps distinctions of language will fade out. Great cities will no longer have reasons for being and will melt away. The men who now dwell in cities will inhabit in summer the mountains and the sea

shores; building often in airy and beautiful spots, now almost or quite inaccessible, commanding the most extensive and magnificent views. In the winter they will probably dwell in communities of moderate size.

Before Socialism crushing toil, cruel anxiety, insulting and demoralizing riches, poverty and its ills will become subjects for historical novels.

In contact with the flux of cosmic consciousness all religions known and named to-day will be melted down. The human soul will be revolutionized. Religion will absolutely dominate the race. . . . Religion will govern every minute of every day of all life. . . . The world peopled by men possessing cosmic consciousness will be as far removed from the world of to-day as this is from the world as it was before the advent of self consciousness (pp. 4–5).

According to Bucke, the evolution of consciousness accounts for the transformation from 'brute to man, from man to demigod' (p. 7). In this evolutionary process there are four distinct stages:

first, the perceptual mind—the mind made up of percepts or sense impressions; second, the mind made up of these and recepts—the so called receptual mind, or in other words the mind of simple consciousness; third, we have the mind made up of percepts, recepts and concepts, called sometimes the conceptual mind or otherwise the self conscious mind—the mind of self consciousness; and, fourth, and last, we have the intuitional mind—the mind whose highest element is not a recept or a concept but an intuition. This is the mind in which sensation, simple consciousness and self consciousness are supplemented and crowned with cosmic consciousness (p. 16).

Of the fourteen extraordinary instances of cosmic consciousness Bucke examines—including Gautama Buddha, Jesus Christ, Paul, Mohammed, and Francis Bacon—Walt Whitman is the most remarkable. Although the terminology has changed from 'moral nature' to 'cosmic consciousness', the psychological phenomena Bucke is describing remain the same: the components of the moral nature are either positive or negative states of *feeling*, and not, as might be expected from traditional ethics, a matter of reason controlling the will. In *Cosmic Consciousness*, Bucke states that he is concerned with 'the evolution of the intellect' (p. 12), but it is clear that in dealing with what he calls the 'intuitions' (p. 16) of cosmic consciousness he is once again dealing with states of feeling.

In several ways *Cosmic Consciousness* is the book Bucke intended to present as Whitman's biography before Whitman began his revisions of the manuscript, deleting Bucke's discussions of the moral nature. Here again Whitman's life and work became both the illustration and the proof of Bucke's theories. Bucke's procedure in rewriting the biography is quite simple. He introduces the biographical section of *Cosmic Consciousness* thus: 'The following brief description is taken from the writer's "Life of Whitman", written in the summer of 1880, while he was visiting the author' (p. 215). The biographical sketch which follows is actually a composite of quotations from *Walt Whitman:*

Bucke begins his analysis by elevating the poet to a supreme position:

> Walt Whitman is the best, most perfect, example the world so far has had of the Cosmic Sense, first because he is the man in whom the new faculty has been, probably, most perfectly developed, and especially because he is, par excellence, the man who in modern times has written distinctly and at large from the point of view of Cosmic Consciousness, and who also has referred to its facts and phenomena more plainly and fully than any other writer either ancient or modern (p. 225).

It was the onset of the faculty of 'cosmic consciousness,' he says, which transformed Whitman from a mere hack into one of the most important writers in the history of the world: 'in the case of Whitman . . . writings of absolutely no value were immediately followed . . . by pages across each of which in letters of ethereal fire are written the words of ETERNAL LIFE. . . . It is upon this instantaneous evolution of the *Titan* from the *Man*, this profound mystery of the attainment of the splendor and power of the kingdom of heaven, that this present volume seeks to throw light' (p. 226).

For biographical evidence of this phenomenon, Bucke selects passages from Whitman's poetry and prose. According to Bucke, Whitman describes his first experience of 'cosmic consciousness' in lines 73–86 of 'Song of Myself' in the 1855 edition of *Leaves of Grass*, which Bucke uses because it brings the reader 'as near the man at the time of writing the words as possible' (p. 227). As in *Walt Whitman*, Bucke quotes a few lines and then presents a commentary and paraphrase in which, ostensibly, the underlying meaning of the text is made clear. Here, however, the text and gloss are presented in parallel columns. The effect, whether intended or not, is that of an annotated edition of the Bible. In the exegesis of the lines he mentions, Bucke finds the following significance: 'The new experience came in June, probably in 1853, when he had just entered upon his thirty-fifth year. It would seem that he was at first in doubt what it meant, then became satisfied and said: I believe in its teaching. Although, however, it is so divine, the other I am (the old self) must not be abased to it, neither must it (the new self) ever be overridden by the more basic organs and faculties' (p. 227).

Bucke's reading of the verse is relentlessly literal, allowing no scope for ambiguity or the complexities of figurative language. For example, Whitman's image of sexual possession (lines 79–81) is reduced to a metaphor of simple dominance:

> You settled your head athwart my hips and gently turned over upon me,
> And parted the shirt from my bosom-bone, and plunged your tongue to my bare-stript heart.
> And reached till you felt my beard, and reached till you held my feet.

Bucke comments: 'His outward life, also, became subject to the dictation of the new self—*it held his feet*' (p. 228).

Whitman differed from all others who experienced 'cosmic consciousness' not only because of the intensity and duration of his intuition, but, most important, because of his ability to integrate this new faculty with the old ones. Whitman 'saw, what neither Guatama nor Paul saw, what Jesus saw, though not so clearly as he, that though this faculty is truly Godlike, yet it is no more supernatural or preternatural than sight, hearing, taste, feeling. . . . He believes in it, but he says the other self, the old self, must not abase itself to the new . . . he will see that they live as friendly co-workers together. And it may here be said that whoever does not realize this last clause will never fully understand the "Leaves" ' (p. 232).

In his analysis of the 'Prayer of Columbus' Bucke feels that Whitman, in the persona of Columbus, finds himself in the situation of a man who, living twenty years under the guidance of 'this (seeming) supernatural illumination' (p. 273), discovers himself to be 'poor, sick, paralyzed, despised, neglected, dying' (p. 233). Yet he continues to trust 'the ray of light, steady, ineffable, with which God has lighted his life; and says it is rare, untellable, beyond all signs, descriptions, languages' (p. 234).

Bucke concludes his examination of Whitman's poetry with a brief commentary on 'To the Sunset Breeze'. In this poem, says Bucke, Whitman bids goodbye to 'cosmic consciousness': 'Doubtless the vision grew more dim and the voice less distinct as time passed and the feebleness of age and sickness advanced upon him. At last, in 1891, at the age of seventy-two, "Brahmic Splendor" finally departed, and in those mystic lines, "To the Sunset Breeze" . . . he bids it farewell!' (p. 235). (Bucke had long felt that he was one of the few to understand this poem.)

In the concluding chapter of his book Bucke's style and method undergo a radical change. Instead of the investigator of psychological phenomena, we find the prophet of new and loftier races of men: 'may it not well be that in the self conscious human being, as we know him to-day, we have the psychic germ of not one higher race only, but of several? . . . As for example: a cosmic conscious race; another race that shall possess seemingly miraculous powers of acting upon what we call objective nature; another with clairvoyant powers far surpassing those possessed by the best specimens so far; another with miraculous healing powers; and so on' (p. 372).

For the mass of men, the keys to these higher states of being are found in the lives and writings of those who have possessed 'cosmic consciousness': 'as one of them [Whitman] says: "I bestow upon any man or woman the entrance to all the gifts of the universe" ' (p. 373). Progress in this direction has been retarded by convention. Rather than accepting the sacred teachings of his particular time and place, each man should seek out what is most meaningful for him: 'And as there are many men in the West who are . . . more benefited by Buddhistic and Mohammedan scriptures than they are by Jewish or Christian, so, doubtless, there are thousands of men in southern Asia who . . . would be . . . more readily and profoundly stirred by the Gospels and Pauline epistles, or "Leaves of Grass" . . . ' (p. 374).

The most remarkable characteristic of this concluding section is the increasingly close identification of Walt Whitman with Christ. However, his achievements as a poet play no essential part in this deification: 'the literary instinct (or expression of any kind) is not necessarily highly developed in the Cosmic Conscious mind, but is a faculty apart. . . . Whitman lived and died vividly conscious of his defects in expression' (p. 375). It is rather his supreme moral development, and other, unnameable qualities, that link Whitman with Gautama and Christ:

> The central point, the kernel of the matter, consists in the fact that they possess qualities for which we at present have no names or concepts. Jesus alluded to one of these when he said: 'Whoever drinketh of the water that I shall give him shall never thirst; but the water that I shall give him shall become in him a well of water springing up unto eternal life.' And Whitman

173

points in the same direction when he declares that his book is not linked with the rest nor felt by the intellect, 'but has to do with untold latencies' in writer and reader, and also when he states that he does not give lectures and charity—that is, either intellectual or moral gifts—but that when he gives he gives himself (pp. 375–76).

In his letters to the other disciples, Bucke was even more explicit in his identification of Whitman with Christ.

Cosmic Consciousness concludes with a millenial vision of a new world peopled by a 'new race': 'The simple truth is, that there has lived on earth, appearing at intervals, for thousands of years among ordinary men, the first faint beginnings of another race; walking the earth and breathing the air with us, but at the same time walking another earth and breathing another air of which we know little or nothing, but which is, all the same, our spiritual life, as its absence would be our spiritual death. This new race is in an act of being born from us, and in the near future it will occupy and possess the earth' (pp. 383–84). No specific details as to how this change will occur are given, but in correspondence with Whitman's other disciples he often mentions this vision.

A few months after the publication of *Cosmic Consciousness*, on 19 February 1902, Bucke died as a result of an accidental fall. He had spent the evening with friends discussing the Bacon-Shakespeare controversy and, upon returning home, 'could not resist the desire to go out once more to look at the night and stars. On the verandah, he slipped, struck his head against a pillar, and dropped lifeless to the floor.'[2]

(103)

To Horace Traubel

2 Jan [18]92

My dear Horace

There was a mail yesterday morning but nothing came

from you—no mail yesterday afternoon—in this mornings mail were three letter (M. & E. of 30th & M. of 31st)—It looks as tho' the dear old man would sink silently into death— but do not feel too sure of this—watch him as closely as you can—it might be that he will brighten up and speak towards the last.—You ought to be in his room when he dies if possible—I wish I could be—if he lives over next week I shall make a strong effort to be there and to keep the doctors on the alert and keep your own eyes open so that I may get such notice of the end as will enable me to be there if possible

If you speak to Walt tell him he is never out of my mind a moment

All good wishes to you
R M Bucke

(104)

To Horace Traubel

11 Jan [18]92

My dear Horace

This morning came to hand yr. letters of thursday eve-ning & 2 written friday—also a bundle of papers con'g pieces re W. W. Many thanks for these last and I do not see why you should not continue to send me such when found in W'^{s} mail as it is hardly likely he will ever want them. My idea now abt. W. is that he will adjust himself to life on a still lower plane than ever heretofore and go on indefinitely—i. e. untill some new attack supervenes— it is really wonderfull—seems as if he *cannot* die—he has been thro' enough to kill several ordinary men. [—] Tell him that I am here and that I never cease to think of him and that he can count on me for this world and the next

Love to you
R M Bucke

175

(105)

To Horace Traubel

15 Jan [18]92

My dear Horace

I have yours of ev'g 12 & m'g 13. I fear W. is suffering a great deal—and I suffer to think of it and because I cannot be with him—I envy you that you at least see him every day and yet I know that you only suffer the more for that. These are terrible days but they cannot surely be much prolonged—but I fear W's almost superhuman strength—there is no telling *what* he may have to pass thro' before the very end. Tell him that I think of him day and night—that he is never out of my thoughts—that he may count on me for this world and all the worlds

Kind & best wishes to Anne & yourself

R M Bucke

(106)

To Horace Traubel

19 Jan [18]92

Dear Horace

I have yours of Saturday evening—also a long letter from Mrs Keller[1] of 17 (Sunday). It seems that a crisis has arisen very different from that which we looked for. Mrs K. writes that W. is so much better that we must look to having him with us "an indefinite time" [/] then she goes on: "It would be impossible to properly clean up the room he is in without removing him to another. The walls are too dusty to touch near his bed. The room is crowded with articles incompatible with a sick room. The bed is infested with bugs and the carpet with moths. Not only the bed but other articles in the room have nits that will next summer produce an army of fresh bugs. The bedstead is an old one, no amount of care would make it fit for an invalid (or any other person) to lie in. His old shirts have been patched untill they are all in tatters, and there is a general lack of every thing. [—] He uses the bedpan usually but at times the bed has to be changed quickly and occasionally the sheets are used much faster than they can be washed and dried. [—] There are no towels, napkins or tray cloths to speak of—neither dishes usually provided for invalids. He needs a bed rest and some other things. [—] Every thing in the house is old and fast falling to pieces. The room Mrs Davis and Warren use (one by night and one by day) is unfit (as it is at present) for human beings. The whole house is unwholesome in the extreme. [—] Insanitary and thoroughly inconvenient. [—] Mr. W. is so wedded to his way of living that I have only made such changes as seemed absolutely necessary that he might be cared for. I have feared to annoy him or put him out. I am now at a loss how to proceed. A complete renovating of the house and a restoring of household effects seems so essential to me.

"Mr. W. is very pleasant and nice to get along with. I feel he is not averse to me or my care. He prefers Warren as a matter of course but I am confident he is as well suited with me as he would be with any outsider. He is comfortable just at present but something must soon be done to give him needed attention—things cannot go on very long as they are—the paper is deserting the walls, the plaster is ready to fall—the water closet is in a miserable state.— [—] Mr Harned is ill today, had he been here I would have said to him what I have written to you."

Now Horace something will have to be done. If a couple of hundred dollars can be raised (over & above Mrs K.'s salary) I would propse to move W. (I do not know that I would even ask his leave—just say it was necessary to move him for a day or so while the room was being fixed up a little) to the next room—then thoroughly clean up and new paper his present room—put a new (iron) bedstead into it and a good set of linen and all necessaries. [—] Put him back into it and renovate the same way Warren's room and the bathroom—for the latter you would have to have the plumbers—plasterer & painter. In this way W's surroundings might be made comfortable and at the same time presentable.[2] Consult H. on this matter as soon as convenient and let me know the result. [—] I have the "American" & "Poet Lore" thanks. [—] I shall read your piece with more care and write about it—Am up to my eyes (and over) in work

Love to Anne

Yours

R M Bucke

[1]Mrs. Elizabeth Leavitt Keller, a professional nurse hired by Bucke to attend to Whitman, tells of her experiences with the poet in *Walt Whitman in Mickle Street* (New York, 1921).
[2]Bucke soon realized that the extensive renovations proposed by Mrs. Keller were not practicable. In a letter to Traubel of 28 January 1892, he proposed more modest arrangements: 'A few dollars for extra bedding and utensils for immediate use such as are needed in /every/ sick room but are not in that sick room (where a divine man lies dying) this seems all that we need think about just now' (Feinberg: LC). At this time Bucke himself had no money to spare. On 1 March 1892, he wrote to Traubel: 'About money matters here—I am infernally hard up—3 boys studing in Toronto and the meter absorbing money as a sandbank absorbs water. Have a little patience with me—I may be good for something (in that line) yet. But at present I am a mere pauper—dead beat. I treat it as a joke but it is getting past a joke. I am in a hole and so mixed up with other people that I cannot stir to get myself out' (Feinberg: LC).

(107)

To Horace Traubel

19 Feb [18]92

My dear Horace

I have your letter of tuesday ev'g. and Wednesday m'g. [—] As to the book ("In re W. W.") I believe our proper course is to *seem to be moving* but *to go slow*. To get out a prospectus—scatter it about pretty well—and let McKay (if he will) have the book announced as to appear "immediately" but I believe what we had better really look forward to is a book *after W's death* to include /(1)/ most of the stuff we have we have [*sic*] in sight now— (2) grave side pieces & (3) any thing else that may crop up—and if we do it this way I would not limit the ed. to 1000 or any definite n° of copies. What we want at present is to *preëmpt* the market. Take possession and keep other "penny a liner" biographies out as much as possible. What I want you to do now is to *amend* and *complete* my prospectus, let me have a look at it and a chance to make suggestions—then get it out and issue it—but with the private understanding that we shall go on with the book *as we can* and *as we think best*

It is snowing again—we have good sleighing and just the most beautifull winter weather you can imagine

We are all well

Tell Walt I never for one minute forget him (I am writing about him at present every spare ½ hour)

Love to Anne
Your friend
R M Bucke

(108)

To Horace Traubel

14 March [18]92

My dear Horace

I have your letter of thursday e'g. and your two letters of friday. [—] I note what you say abt. W. not being able to lie on his back nor right side more than 5 minutes and the left side being sore to lie on. Had I a patient in such a fix as this I should put him on a *water bed*—and on that he could lie on his *back*—& so could W. If the case is really as bad as seems from your letter a water bed should be procured at once. /Will you speak to Longaker?/[1] Do you think W. would tell you any thing about his own experience of "Cosmic Consciousness"? Would you try him some day if he was in better trim than usual? Do not say that I asked you. Tell him (for instance) that the doctor says that Christ, Paul & Mohamet all had C. C. but that W. W. is the man

179

who has had it in most pronounced development—then try and get from /ask/ him something about it [/] where he was and what doing at the time /it first made its appearance/? Did a luminous haze accompany the onset of C. C.? How many times has the C. C. returned? and how long remained at a time?

If you could quietly induce W. to talk about this experience it will be /It would be/ most important to me and interesting to thousands—to many millions in the end, but I fear he will say nothing. If I had known as much a few years ago (abt C. C.) as I do now I would have got some valuable statements from him but now I fear it is too late[2]

Tell Walt that my heart is with him there in Camden always and always

---

[1]Dr. Daniel Longaker attended Whitman in his last illness; his account 'The Last Sickness and the Death of Walt Whitman', is found in *In Re Walt Whitman*, pp. 393–411.

[2]It is apparent that Whitman never outlined for Bucke the specific details of his mystical experience—if, indeed, there had ever been one. Realizing that the opportunity to question Whitman was quickly passing, Bucke was anxious not to let it slip by.

(109)

To Horace Traubel

18 March [18]92

My dear Horace

I have yours of e'g. & night 15th & m'g. 16th[.] This is heartbreaking work—to have Walt lying suffering as he is and not able to do the last thing for him. But it is more and more clear to me that he ought at once to have a *water bed*. He could probably lie on such a bed on his back or left side *continuously*—and might sleep.[1]

All well here—I am 55 today—do not feel any the worse for it so far! It is a grand thing to be getting on well towards the end without serious demoralization in any direction!

About the worst thing in the world is to see a decent man thro' disease or defective heredity break down morally towards the end /&/ leave his memory stained & blurred

Love to Anne—So long!
R M Bucke

[1]Apparently Whitman had some objections to the water bed. On 22 March 1892, Bucke wrote Traubel: '—of course he will "kick" at the water bed (he does at every thing) but let him lie on one for twenty four hours and I am confident he would acknowledge its virtues' (Feinberg: LC). And on 25 March 1892, when the water bed had been procured, Bucke wrote Traubel: 'If W. does not like the W. bed at first make him stick to it—he *will* like it—can't help—but it is queer to lie on at first' (Feinberg: LC).

(110)

To Horace Traubel

March 20th, 1892

strictly *private*

My dear Horace:—

As you know I am writing on what I call "Cosmic Consciousness". Of all men who have ever lived I believe Walt Whitman has had this faculty most perfectly developed. I am anxious therefore to obtain from him some confirmation or some correction of my views on the subject and I ask you to read this letter to him and get from him if possible answers (however brief) to the series of questions with which it ends.

1 The human mind is made up of a great many faculties and these are of all ages some dating back millions or many millions of years, other only thousands of years, others like the musical sense just coming into existence.

2 As main trunk and stem of all the faculties are /1/ consciousness and /2/ self consciousness the one many million[s] of years old the other dating back perhaps a few hundred thousand years.

3 What I claim is that a third stage of consciousness is now coming into existence, and that I call "C. C."

4 Of course when a new faculty comes into existence in any race at first one individual has it, then as the generations succeed one another more and more individuals have it until after say a thousand generations it beomes general in the race.

5 "C. C." dates back at least to the time of Buddha—it was this faculty that came to him under the Bo tree some two thousand five hundred years ago.

6 Christ certainly had the faculty though we have no record of how and when it came to him.

7 St Paul and Mohammed had it and we have pretty full details in both these cases of the time and manner of its onset, and we can plainly trace the effects of their illumination in their writings. P. refers to faculty fully & explicitly[.]

8 The faculty seems to be much commoner now than it used to be. I know six men who have had it in more or less pronounced development. N. B. A man may have it for half a minute or off & on for years & for days continuously[.]

9 Whatever Walt may say to you about it every page of L. of G. proves the possession of the faculty by the writer.

10 Not only so but he describes the onset of the faculty, its results and its passing away, and directly alludes to it over and over again.

11 The faculty always comes suddenly—it came to W. suddenly one June day between the years 1850 and 1855—which year was it?

12 Was the onset of the faculty accompanied by a sensation of physical illumination? As if he were in the midst of a great flame? or as if a bright light shown in his mind?

13 What did he think of the new comer at first? Was he alarmed? Did he think (or fear) he was becoming insane?

14 Here follows /15–16 &c./ a brief description of the onset of "C. C."—is it fairly accurate or will Walt suggest some alterations or additions?

15 The man suddenly, without warning, has a sense of being immersed in a flame or rose colored cloud or haze—or perhaps rather a sense that the mind itself is filled with such a haze.

16 At the same instant or immediately afterwards he is bathed in an emotion of joy, exultation, triumph.

17 Along with this is what must be called for want of better words a sense of immortality and accompanying this:—

18 A clear conception (in outline) of the drift of the universe—a consciousness that the central over-ruling power is infinitely beneficient, also:—

19 An intellectual competency not simply surpassing the old but on a new and higher plane.

Just as science rests on reason, just as society rests on love and friendship, and is high or low according to the presence or absence of these, so religion rests on "C. C."

It may be said indeed in a very true sense that all that is best /in/ modern civilization depends on the light that has /shone/ by means of this faculty on half a dozen men—of these few men W. W. I believe is really chief and on him will rest a higher civilization than we have yet known—but meanwhile (while this is building) "C. C." will become more and more common, and *his* prophesy of other and greater /bards/ will be fulfilled and by means of the spread of the same faculty an audience will be supplied which will be worthy of its poets.

Tell W. that I beg of him to give me through you a little light to help me forward with my present task.[1]

With love to W. and to all his friends,
R M Bucke

---

[1]From Bucke's subsequent letters to Traubel and from his essays on 'cosmic consciousness', it would appear that Traubel never posed these questions to Whitman; at least, if he did, Whitman did not answer. Whitman's last words, as reported by Mrs. Keller, were practical. Because it was painful for him to lie in one position for any period of time, he had to be turned on his water bed frequently, and his last words, addressed to Warren Fritzinger, were 'Shift, Warry' (Keller, *Walt Whitman*, p. 175)

(111)

To J. W. Wallace and John Johnston

10 April [18]92

Dear Wallace and Johnston

Many thanks for your good kind letters. [—] I cannot write to you yet—my heart is as heavy as lead.[1] But it will pass off and please God we will work for dear Walt harder than ever. [—] Over and over again I keep saying to myself: The Christ is dead! Again we have buried the Christ! And for the time there seems to be an end of every thing. But I *know* he is not dead and I *know* that this pain will pass. Give my love to all the dear College fellows—*now* we are really brothers

God bless you all
R M Bucke

[1]Whitman died on 26 March.

(112)

To J. W. Wallace

24 June [18]93

Dear Wallace

The notes on "Walt Whitman's Birthday" meeting in Bolton last 31st May are just to hand sent to me by kindness of some of the "boys"—probably my good friend Dixon— hearty thanks to him and to all! I never doubted, my dear friend, that *you* at least realized (as much as is possible at this early date) what Walt's life, work and death means for us—his followers and disciples—none the less I was deeply interested & pleased to read your own words fully setting forth your own appreciation of your (of our) position. [—] You know well that we here (a few at least) feel with you in this matter and that we are working—and (please God) shall work with all the strength and energy that is in us to accomplish the task before us. [—] For my part (I have said it before) my life has been dedicated for now many years to the "Great Cause" and what remains of it is and shall be also so dedicated. It is the one thing I care for—that I live for and if I could in some way die for it I think my satisfaction would be complete. [—] To all of you, then, —devoted friends of our dear friend recognition, sympathy, love now and always from your lover and fellow laborer

R M Bucke

(113)

To J. W. Wallace

25 March [18]94

Dear Wallace

"Christ ist erstanden!" More correctly he is arising. I should have answered yours of 2 of Dec. before now by rights but I sit here and turn the handle of this mill untill I become a sort of a machine myself. I think I should go quite to sleep (and perhaps a very good thing too!) were it not for my book—an occational hour at it gives me renewed interest in life and the world. I am glad to find that you have tackled the current social problems *in ernest*—there is unlimited work waiting *now* to be done. We are entering (have entered?) one of the most tremendous crises in history and, as meterologists say, the "central depression" seems to be over England.[1] Should I live ten years longer I look to see immense changes—the Lords must go almost at once—the throne will soon follow—the church must be disestablished *every where*—these changes *will introduce* the revolution. When *this* really comes we shall have nationalization of the mines, railways, land—the present useless and worse than useless drones who have too long lived on the labor of others and have rewarded others—their betters—by affecting to look down upon them—these drones must work or die—the rightfull owner (the creator) of English civilization and its products must enter into his inheritance. [—] Do not forget that I shall be glad of any hints you may feel to give me on the subject of C. C. as this is (of course) *the* subject with me now. The few pages in "In Re" are too fragmentary to be of any account one way or the other—I published them as a miner *stakes his claim*—to notify all and sundry that I had *taken up the land.*

Do not let the College boys forget me—I shall drop in upon you one of these days and when I do I shall hunt them all up—give my love to D^r and Mrs Johnston

I am, dear Wallace, affectionately yours

R M Bucke

The meter is moving forwards—we have begun manufacturing here—we think we have it *right* this time and if so it will make some money for us.

So long!

R M B

---

[1]Bucke outlined some of these revolutionary changes in *Cosmic Consciousness* (see pp. 4–5).

(114)

To C. F. Sixsmith

1st May 1894

My dear Sixsmith

Very many thanks for "New Review" with Gosse's W. W. piece which of course I wanted and did not know where to get when your gift came along and filled up the gap.[1] I am very glad that you are with Wallace and that you know enough to appreciate him. Wallace is one of "the coming race" an expression which you will appreciate better when you read a little paper of mine which I hope to send you in a few weeks. Carpenter is another and even better marked specimen of what some American friends of mine call (not Christians but) "Christ-men". You, I hope, too, are there or on the road. Yes I read all Carpenter's books and never get enough of them. So I read them over again when the interval is too long to wait from one to the other.

I am writing a book now that you will like, I wish it was ready but it will not be for a year or two—it is to be called "Cosmic Consciousness" and will be a good sized volume.

Give my love to Wallace

    do   do   Carpenter

    do   do   Ned Wild and all the College boys.

Love to you, too, my dear boy

R. M. Bucke.

[1]Edmund Gosse, 'A Note on Walt Whitman', *New Review,* 10 (April 1894), 447.

6

Conclusion

True appreciation of Bucke's relationship to Whitman must be founded on an understanding of the essentially religious nature of his discipleship. For Bucke, Whitman was, quite literally, the Messiah. In his writings and person, Bucke had discovered his own salvation, and much of the extravagance and dogmatism of his pronouncements is explained if it is seen as the testimony of the man who has found his saviour. Yet Bucke's devotion had more focus and direction than that of the usual religious enthusiast: it had a historic precedent.

In the opening pages of *Cosmic Consciousness* Bucke sets

188

up an equation: 'The Saviour of man is Cosmic Consciousness—in Paul's language—the Christ' (p. 6). Bucke's glos-
ses on Paul's epistle to the Galatians revealed to him that
for Paul Christ was the Messiah because in Him he had
recognized the teachings of cosmic consciousness: 'He
[Paul] knew, however, enough about Jesus and his teachings to be able to recognize (when it came to him) that the
teachings of the Cosmic Sense were practically identical
with the teachings of Jesus' (p. 116). Indeed, Christ is cosmic consciousness made flesh: 'Christ is the Cosmic Sense
conceived as a distinct entity or individuality' (p. 116). The
relationship between Paul and Christ thus becomes a
prototype rather than a unique historical event. As the evolutionary process continues, any man who embodies the
intentions of cosmic consciousness is Christ, and any who
follows him for the sake of his wisdom is Paul. If we follow
this process to its limit, we find that since Whitman is
superior to Christ, Bucke must be superior to Paul.

In Paul, Bucke also finds his defense against the scorn of
the world. He quotes the apostle's famous paradox: 'If any
man thinketh that he is wise among you in this world, let
him become a fool, that he may become wise. For the wisdom of this world is foolishness with God' (1 Corinthians
3:18–19). Bucke explains the statement in terms of cosmic
consciousness: 'Paul says the wisdom of self consciousness
is not the wisdom of those who have the Cosmic Sense,
and the wisdom of the latter is foolishness to the merely
self conscious' (p. 117).

Bucke's exalted view of his devotion to Whitman, of
course, met with little understanding. To his friends, it
was an embarrassment; and to the less sympathetic, it
was ridiculous. Bucke's devotion is recorded in an anec-
dote. Sir William Osler, a friend of Bucke, recalls the following incident.

> One evening after dinner . . . I drew Bucke on to tell the story of
> Whitman's influence. . . . It was an experience to hear an elderly

189

man—looking a venerable seer—with absolute abandonment tell how "Leaves of Grass" had meant for him spiritual enlightenment, a new power in life, new joys in a new existence on a plane higher than he had ever hoped to reach. All this with the accompanying physical exaltation expressed by dilated pupils and intensity of utterance that were embarrassing to uninitiated friends.[1]

What appears excessive and even ludicrous in a literary disciple is acceptable and commendable in a religious one. Like Paul, Bucke depended on the divinity of his messiah to justify his faith. In his first epistle to the Corinthians, Paul announced: 'And if Christ be not raised, your faith is in vain!' (15:17). Because Christians have accepted the divinity of Christ, Paul's faith has been justified by history, but the reputation of Whitman, despite his unquestioned eminence as a poet, has provided no such support for Bucke's belief. Claims for his divinity are treated as at best metaphorical and at worst as absurd.

But the position of Bucke among Whitman's disciples is central. From his letters and published writings it may be seen that his devotion was coherent and even noble. He attempted to satisfy his need for a living Messiah by finding in Whitman a contemporary sacred presence and in *Leaves of Grass* an addition to the canon of the world's sacred texts. These convictions led him not only to render great personal services to Whitman but to bring together many scattered enthusiasts into a solid band of Whitmanites. It was Bucke who was in large part responsible for organizing that 'great audience' which Whitman so craved.

notes

Chapter One

1. The basic source for Bucke's life is James H. Coyne's *Richard Maurice Bucke: A Sketch* (Toronto, 1923).
2. *Cosmic Consciousness: A Study in the Evolution of the Human Mind* (Philadelphia, 1901), p. 8.
3. Ibid.
4. Bucke wrote an interesting account of his western adventures in 'Twenty-Five Years Ago', *Overland Monthly*, 1, 2d ser. (June 1883), 553–60.
5. *British American Journal*, 3 (1862), 161–67, 225–38.
6. MS (Weldon).
7. MS (Weldon).
8. 'Memories of Walt Whitman', *Walt Whitman Fellowship Papers*, No. 6, p. 35 (September 1894). This was originally presented as a paper at the Walt Whitman Fellowship annual meeting on 31 May 1894.
9. Seaborn typescript (Weldon).
10. 18 March 1869 (MS, Weldon).
11. 11 April 1869 (Seaborn typescript, Weldon).
12. MS (Weldon).
13. Seaborn typescript (Weldon).
14. 1–13 April 1869 (Seaborn typescript, Weldon).
15. 13 March 1872 (Seaborn typescript, Weldon).
16. 19 March 1872 (Seaborn typescript, Weldon).
17. Pp. 9–10.
18. 11 September 1871 (Seaborn typescript, Weldon).
19. 11 December 1871 (Seaborn typescript, Weldon).
20. 10 December 1872 (Seaborn typescript, Weldon).
21. 18 June 1873 (Seaborn typescript, Weldon).

22. 17 February 1875 (Seaborn typescript, Weldon).
23. 'The Function of the Great Sympathetic Nervous System', *American Journal of Insanity*, 34 (October 1877), 115–59; 'The Moral Nature and the Great Sympathetic', *American Journal of Insanity*, 35 (October 1878), 229–53, reprinted in the same year as a pamphlet under the same title by Ellis H. Roberts of Utica, N.Y. Both were first presented as papers before annual meetings of the Association of Medical Superintendents of American Institutions for the Insane.
24. Bucke to H. B. Forman, 2 February and 20 May 1876 (Seaborn typescripts, Weldon).

Chapter Two

1. P. 37.
2. *Walt Whitman* (Philadelphia, 1883), p. 50.
3. *Calamus. A Series of Letters Written during the Years 1868–1880. By Walt Whitman to a Young Friend (Peter Doyle)* (Boston, 1897), p. 12.
4. P. 37.
5. Seaborn typescript (Weldon).
6. *Man's Moral Nature: An Essay* (New York, 1879), pp. 76–79.
7. *Days with Walt Whitman* (London, 1906), pp. 61–62.

Chapter Three

1. London *Advertiser*, 5 June 1880.
2. 'Summer Days in Canada' (22 June 1880), 'Letter from Walt Whitman [on St. Lawrence River Trip]' (26 August 1880), and 'Walt Whitman Safe Home' (4 October 1880).
3. Edwin Haviland Miller, ed., *Walt Whitman: The Correspondence*, vol. 3 (New York: New York University Press, 1964), 339n. The artist was Herbert H. Gilchrist.
4. Bucke not only reprints Emerson's letter of 7 December 1856 concerning the first edition, and Thoreau's letter of 7 December 1856 concerning the second, but also points out what a good financial investment the centennial edition is: 'The total number of pages is 734, and the total number of poems 288. Each volume contains the author's autograph, and the two books include three portraits. It will not be many years before copies of this Centennial edition will bring almost anything that holders of them like to ask' (p. 146).
5. Bucke is quoting from bk. 1, ll. 591–93, of Milton's *Paradise Lost*.
6. Seaborn typescript (Weldon).

Chapter Four

1. *At the Graveside of Walt Whitman: Harleigh, Camden, New Jersey, March 30th and Sprigs of Lilac* (Philadelphia, 1892), reprinted in part in *In Re Walt Whitman*, ed. Horace L. Traubel, Richard Maurice Bucke, and Thomas Harned (Philadelphia, 1893), pp. 437–52.
2. *In Re*, p. 448.
3. Seaborn typescript (Weldon).
4. 23 February 1896 (MS, Bolton).

5. 'American Literature', *Literature*, 2 (16 April 1898), 453, reprinted in Milton Hindus, ed., *Walt Whitman: The Critical Heritage* (New York, 1971), p. 260.
6. *The Wound Dresser. A Series of Letters Written from the Hospitals in Washington during the War of Rebellion by Walt Whitman*, ed. Richard Maurice Bucke, (Boston, 1898).
7. MS (Feinberg: LC).
8. 12 February 1898 (Seaborn typescript, Weldon).
9. 4 February 1898 (MS, Feinberg: LC).
10. *Notes and Fragments*, ed. Richard Maurice Bucke (London, Ontario, 1899) (privately printed).
11. Feinberg: LC.
12. MS (Feinberg: LC).
13. MS (Feinberg: LC).
14. MS (Feinberg: LC).
15. Carolyn Wells and Alfred F. Goldsmith, *A Concise Bibliography of the Works of Walt Whitman* (Boston and New York, 1922), p. 42.
16. *The Complete Writings of Walt Whitman*, 10 vols. (New York and London, 1902).

Chapter Five

1. Seaborn typescript (Weldon).
2. Coyne, *Bucke*, p. 67.

Chapter Six

1. Quoted in Harvey Cushing, *The Life of Sir William Osler* (London, 1940), p. 266.

abbreviations

Bolton	County Borough of Bolton (England) Public Libraries.
CB	'The Commonplace-Book', Feinberg: LC.
Corr.	*The Collected Writings of Walt Whitman: The Correspondence.* Edited by Edwin Haviland Miller. 5 vols. New York: New York University Press, 1961–69.
Coyne	James H. Coyne. *Richard Maurice Bucke: A Sketch.* Toronto: Henry S. Saunders, 1923.
Feinberg: LC	The Charles E. Feinberg Whitman Collection at the Library of Congress.
In Re	*In Re Walt Whitman.* Edited by Horace L. Traubel, Richard Maurice Bucke, and Thomas B. Harned. Philadelphia: David McKay, 1893.
Johnston and Wallace	John Johnston and J. W. Wallace. *Visits to Walt Whitman in 1890–91. By Two Lancashire Friends.* London: G. Allen & Unwin, 1918.
LC	Library of Congress, Washington, D.C.
Manchester	The John Rylands Library, Manchester, England.
Schueller and Peters	*The Letters of John Addington Symonds.* Edited by Herbert M. Schueller and Robert L. Peters. 3 vols. Detroit: Wayne State University Press, 1967–69.
Seaborn	Edwin Seaborn typescripts of Bucke papers (Weldon).

Abbreviations

Syracuse   Syracuse University Library

Traubel   Horace L. Traubel. *With Walt Whitman in Camden.* Vol. 1: *March 28–July 14, 1888* (Boston: Small, Maynard and Co., 1906); Vol. 2: *July 16–October 31, 1888* (New York: D. Appleton and Co., 1908); Vol. 3: *November 1– January 20, 1889* (New York: Mitchell Kennerley, 1914); Vol. 4: *January 21–April 7, 1889,* ed. Sculley Bradley (Carbondale: Southern Illinois University Press, 1959); Vol. 5: *April 8–September 14, 1889,* ed. Gertrude Traubel (Carbondale: Southern Illinois University Press, 1964).

Weldon   D. B. Weldon Library, University of Western Ontario, London, Ontario.

WW   precedes number of Whitman letter in *Corr.*

196

manuscript
sources

Letter	Collection	Letter	Collection
1	Feinberg: LC	25	Feinberg: LC
2	Weldon	26	Feinberg: LC
3	Seaborn	27	Feinberg: LC
4	Feinberg: LC	28	Feinberg: LC
5	Weldon	29	Feinberg: LC
6	Seaborn	30	Feinberg: LC
7	Seaborn	31	Feinberg: LC
8	Manchester	32	Feinberg: LC
9	Manchester	33	Feinberg: LC
10	Weldon	34	Feinberg: LC
11	Seaborn	35	Feinberg: LC
12	Weldon	36	Feinberg: LC
13	Seaborn	37	Feinberg: LC
14	Seaborn	38	Feinberg: LC
15	Weldon	39	Feinberg: LC
16	Feinberg: LC	40	Feinberg: LC
17	LC	41	Feinberg: LC
18	Feinberg: LC	42	Feinberg: LC
19	Feinberg: LC	43	Feinberg: LC
20	Seaborn	44	Feinberg: LC
21	Feinberg: LC	45	Feinberg: LC
22	Feinberg: LC	46	Feinberg: LC
23	Feinberg: LC	47	Feinberg: LC
24	Feinberg: LC	48	Feinberg: LC

Manuscript Sources

Letter	Collection	Letter	Collection
49	Syracuse	76	Feinberg: LC
50	Feinberg: LC	77	Feinberg: LC
51	Feinberg: LC	78	Feinberg: LC
52	Feinberg: LC	79	Feinberg: LC
53	Feinberg: LC	80	Feinberg: LC
54	Feinberg: LC	81	Feinberg: LC
55	Feinberg: LC	82	Bolton
56	Feinberg: LC	83	Feinberg: LC
57	Feinberg: LC	84	Feinberg: LC
58	Feinberg: LC	85	Feinberg: LC
59	Feinberg: LC	86	Feinberg: LC
60	Feinberg: LC	87	Feinberg: LC
61	Feinberg: LC	88	Bolton
62	Seaborn	89	Feinberg: LC
63	Feinberg: LC	90	Bolton
64	Feinberg: LC	91	Feinberg: LC
65	Feinberg: LC	92	Feinberg: LC
66	Feinberg: LC	93	Feinberg: LC
67	Feinberg: LC	94	Feinberg: LC
68	Feinberg: LC	95	Feinberg: LC
69	Feinberg: LC	96	Feinberg: LC
70	Bolton	97	Feinberg: LC
71	Feinberg: LC	98	Feinberg: LC
72	Feinberg: LC	99	Bolton
73	Feinberg: LC	100	Bolton
74	Feinberg: LC	101	Bolton
75	Feinberg: LC	102	Bolton

index

Index

Dr. Richard Maurice Bucke (1837–1902) was one of the most remarkable Canadians of the nineteenth century. A psychiatrist, a mystic, and a disciple and friend of Walt Whitman, he perceived in Whitman the supreme example of what he called 'cosmic consciousness'. Through his interest in philosophy and mysticism he developed a relationship with Whitman which became a life-long devotion, and these letters reflect the growth of that discipleship. The letters of Whitman to Bucke have been available for several years; with the publication of this volume the reader can now follow both sides of this remarkable exchange.

An annotated edition of Bucke's collected letters to Whitman, which also contains a selected bibliography of Bucke's writings, is published simultaneously with this volume and is available through the Xerox University Microfilms *Monograph Publishing On Demand* program.

Artem Lozynsky received the Ph.D. degree from Wayne State University. He is on the faculty of the English Department at Temple University.

The manuscript was prepared for publication by Jean Owen. The book was designed by Donald Ross. The face for the text and display is Palatino, designed by Hermann Zapf about 1950. The text is printed on Glatfelter Natural paper and the book is bound in Joanna Mills' Linson #2 and Joanna Mills' Kennett cloth over boards. Manufactured in the United States of America.